CAPITAL CRUSADERS

LONG TERM PLANNING TO
LEGALLY REDUCE YOUR TAXES
EVERY YEAR

MARDIS ★ DALLAS

DEDICATION

*For all the hard-working American patriots
in search of a better way.*

About the Authors

Walt Dallas
Co-Author

As a tax attorney, I have the opportunity to assist clients on many different levels. These levels have included estate tax planning, asset protection, business succession planning, and obviously income tax planning.

As a young attorney, I was introduced to real income tax planning in the 1990s by a group called Fortress Financial Group. This group was comprised of tax attorneys, CPAs, and some of the country's top financial planners. The lesson learned was with planning and thinking outside the box, as there are a great deal of opportunities for legal tax reduction. Many of these opportunities begin with a proper corporate structure.

The strategic alliance with Todd and Capital Preservation

Services has allowed me to share these processes and techniques with successful business owners on a national level.

I have written and co-authored several books including: *The Complete Guide to Estate and Financial Planning in Turbulent Times* and *How to Pay Less in U.S. Taxes: Change Your Facts to Change Your Tax*. This book, *Capital Crusaders*, is a very informative book that offers the reader a great deal of insight into true tax planning but in a way that does not include a lot of advanced legal terminology.

TODD MARDIS
CO-AUTHOR

I began in the financial service industry in 1993 with Revere Financial Services. I was straight out of college and had little to no experience in the world of finance other than a few college courses.

I had the benefit of working with Gerald Sartin and Bruce Sartin. These two individuals had as much impact on me professionally then as they do now. They taught me the importance of learning at a deep level any product or service I offered. They emphasized filling a "hole" for the client's financial portfolio, and everything else would fall in place.

Over the next twenty-eight years my practice evolved into filling a hole, which was focused on reducing income taxes for successful business owners. This evolution was completed in 2009 when I strategically partnered with Walt Dallas, the book's co-author. Over the last eleven years, Capital Preservation Services has expanded into a national consulting firm with clients in forty-six states. CPS has partnered with multiple national professional associations and continues to grow. Our success is built on service as much as it is black letter tax codes.

This book is written in a conversational form, and the intent is to provide insight into high-level tax planning processes without putting the reader straight to sleep.

DONALD TRUMP

"I HOPE WE NEVER FIND LIFE
ON OTHER PLANETS, BECAUSE IF WE DO
THE UNITED STATES GOVERNMENT
WILL START SENDING THEM
MONEY."

INTRODUCTION

TODD: I'm not a CPA, nor am I an attorney. Like many of the people reading this book, I'm a successful business owner with a lot of practical knowledge and expertise I've amassed over several decades. Over time, as my different ventures grew, I watched my federal taxes skyrocket. It was clear that the better we did and the more income we brought in, there was only one place for those taxes to go. That was up, to the next bracket and the next.

Frustrated, I began searching for ways to lower the amount—completely legally—that I would pay the federal government each year. That search brought me to attorney Walt Dallas, who knows the U.S. Tax Code inside and out and provided solid, reliable answers rooted in common sense.

WALT: Unlike Todd, I am an attorney with a Master's in Taxation and I have been practicing for over thirty-five years in the area of tax. Like Todd, I have always recognized American business people's frustration with ever-increasing taxes. Fortunately, I knew there were solid solutions available and clearly spelled out in the U.S. tax code. I have enjoyed working with my friend Todd Mardis because he brings a practical understanding of tax code strategies with a remarkable talent of explaining complex matters. Sometimes tax professionals, including me, are difficult to understand, and Todd bridges that gap.

TODD: With that in mind, let me ask a question: Who among us looks forward to paying taxes?

Don't misunderstand—everyone should do so. You'll hear me say that often. I want clean air and water, safe roads and bridges, well-staffed police and fire departments, and quality public education just as much as you. Our hard-earned money from which our taxes are paid goes to all of those things.

The hard truth, though, is that fifty percent of the people in this country pay no taxes at all. Not only are you shouldering a hefty tax burden if you're running a successful company, you're most likely choosing to pay more in taxes by not reading the rule book—or having someone qualified to help you do so.

That rule book, of course, is our country's tax code. It's literally thousands of pages long. Who has time to read such a thing while running a company? The politicians in Washington successfully crafted the Tax Code to make sure it benefits them, and you can bet your last dollar that people like Warren Buffett and Jeff Bezos insist on being made aware of every rule in the Code that applies to their investments and holdings. Why?

Because it benefits them to do so. Just as it will benefit you.

No, you don't have time to read the entire tax code and stay current on it. Nor do Buffett and Bezos, but they and many other sophisticated business owners and investors arm themselves with weapons most people don't have, like tax specialists who know the rule book inside and out.

We provide you with Walt and arm you with the knowledge—based on your assets and what you tell us you want to accomplish with them—to make your own out-of-the-box investing decisions going forward. We empower you to grow your nest egg in ways you never dreamed, and ways that probably never occurred to your CPA.

WALT: Tax deductions are written into the Code in legislative action. They may not be extremely logical because there's usually a lobbyist or well-financed company (or both) behind the formation of the tax break. But the good news is that these tax breaks are for all . . . if you know how to use them.

TODD: In that vein, your CPA (probably a fine person and imminently qualified to file your taxes), typically reports to the IRS what has already happened. There's no proactive thinking, there. We, however, work with you—and think with you—ahead of time to structure your assets to more properly fit the rules of the Tax Code. We'll not only show you what to look for, we'll educate you in ways that will have you looking through the big rule book for completely legal avenues of minimizing your federal tax burden.

***

TODD: Again, everyone should pay taxes. Those that falsify information or just flat out don't pay what they owe should be prosecuted to the fullest extent the law allows. Conversely, what you've earned is your money. Yes, you're paying taxes on it. That's how our system works. But why not try to learn every legal way you can to decrease what you owe, by learning to do what some of the wealthiest and most sophisticated investors in America do each day? To put a finer point on it, this is about more than just lowering your federal tax burden—it's about avoiding overpaying. If you're running a very successful company, you're already paying a significant amount to the U.S. government. Why pay a nickel more than you have to?

Let me bring this to life a bit more. A man we'll call Frank is a successful optometrist. He has five locations within a radius of two hundred miles. A hard-working, second-generation specialist who has built a proven practice, Frank runs a small company with approximately forty employees. His federal tax bill grew to roughly $200,000 last year.

I can get it down to $125,000 with ease—while doing so completely legally.

WALT: One of the fundamental understandings Todd and I have is that any strategy must meet the tests in the Internal Revenue Service code, compliant with code sections like 7701(o), which generally requires an independent business purpose for any transaction, and section 162, which requires a deduction to be ordinary, necessary, and reasonable. Todd and I built our relationship on this understanding, and it permeates throughout our service to clients.

TODD: Let's say you and your CPA, a decade ago, agreed on a C corporation when you launched your business. Over the last ten years, you've paid taxes on the income your business has made as well as taxes on the income you've received as an owner. Your company has done very well over the last five years, and you're projecting an equally-strong next five years. Since the start-up, you have three additional investors and a dozen new employees. All of that is positive.

Your federal tax burden, however, is soaring each year.

We might suggest you move from the C Corporation to an S Corporation, explaining that an S corporation doesn't pay tax on business revenue—you and the other owners would report the company revenue as personal income. That's completely legal, in case you're wondering. So why aren't more people in your shoes doing exactly that?

Because they don't know to do so.

Let's go back to the $75,000 savings on Frank's federal tax bill. What might Frank want to do with those funds? Purchase a new car? Make it part of a down payment on a new home? On the business side, he could probably hire two or even three employees, depending on responsibilities and experience required. Or he might want to reinvest.

We can help Frank—and you—do all of that, and we're not talking about a one-time savings. We have many clients like Frank who, in round numbers, have saved close to a million dollars in federal taxes over the last decade. What could Frank do with that kind of money?

What could you do with it?

***

TODD: Walt is a close friend of mine as well as a trusted business partner. He and I give many talks together and enjoy playing off each other, as well as being able to address questions and issues all over the broad financial planning and tax consultation spectrum. We will be along for the entire journey as we get you ready to scrape every penny away from your tax burden allowable by law.

This sounds exciting, doesn't it? Then what are we waiting for? Let's get started.

RONALD REAGAN

"THE AMERICAN PEOPLE
ARE NOT OVERTAXED,
THE GOVERNMENT IN WASHINGTON
IS OVERFED."

WHO WILL BENEFIT FROM THE TECHNIQUES IN THIS BOOK?

Walt: If you are reading this book, chances are, you are looking for ways to reduce your tax liability. Generally, the kind of tax planning we will discuss in this book will help people more when they reach a specific income threshold. It would be best if you had a certain level of income to work with, and you also need control over how income is paid to you on a business level. If you own a business and earn over $350,000 a year, the concepts explained in this book will be beneficial to you. If you earn less, the tax rates are too low, and our level of tax planning will not make sense. Once the income is paid out to an individual and becomes taxable on a 1040 form, it becomes challenging to take advantage of the Internal Revenue Code deductions.

Todd: Like Walt referenced, for us to really help, income levels need to be more than $350,000. Under this income level, a person who is married filing jointly would be in a 24% bracket. That means the person would be in the range of $320,000 of taxable income, which is a pretty good place to be. However, when someone jumps to a 32% bracket, we can really apply our techniques.

Walt: Our techniques work especially well in that context. No matter what kind of business, this book will help if you are in the right bracket. We have clients from various industries – from heavy equipment operators to orthopedic and brain surgeons and everyone in between. We do not have an occupation-specific planning process. You just need to meet an income threshold and can control how it is paid.

Todd: That is the key point. It is best to use your money for things other than a traditional salary. If someone is employed by a hospital and is receiving a W2, these techniques will not work as well. There are exceptions, of course. For instance, if you are a physician at a hospital earning $400,000 a year, a few of these concepts may work for you.

Walt: As Todd mentioned, there are a few techniques and strategies that work for super-high earners who are W2 employees, but the planning is a lot more limited in that context. For instance, you could be a W2 employee and still participate in conservation easements. For the most part, if you want to take advantage of these deductions, you need to be self-employed. You will have the flexibility to take advantage of the deductions the Code offers, which can provide you significant tax savings. For example, we worked with a dentist in Birmingham, Alabama. He is a sole practitioner who operates with 4-5 employees. With strategic planning and coaching, we increased his income from roughly $350,000 to around $500,000 - but we dropped his effective rate from close to 35% down to 18%. We did this over six months by creating the right structures, implementing the right strategies, and positioning the right people in the right places.

Todd: When most clients come on board with us, they have an effective federal and state rate somewhere between 35-42%, depending on the state rate. Once we apply our strategies, though, their effective rate drops to between 17-22%.

One of our clients is an artist in Georgia who earns around a million dollars a year. We organized a series of strategies that allowed him to use the new qualified business income deduction - which meant we reduced his taxable income below $331,000. It is unusual to move someone from a million in taxable income to a third of the total, but when everything clicks like it's supposed to, you can see outstanding results.

Walt: That was a fantastic result. A few of our clients, who earn $400,000-$500,000, were able to reduce their effective tax rate down as low as 15%. However, it is challenging for many high-income earners to move them below about 20%. As a rule, we typically do not like reducing our clients' effective tax rate below 15%. It can be achieved using our strategies, but we have a firm philosophy. We believe everyone needs to pay their fair share of taxes.

> "AS A RULE, WE DON'T LIKE GETTING OUR CLIENTS BELOW A 10 PERCENT EFFECTIVE RATE"
>
> WALT DALLAS

Todd: We all enjoy clean air, good schools, and nice roads, so we believe everyone should pay their fair share of taxes. When I am creating proposals, I look at different strategies. If a particular strategy pushes someone below 15%, I reduce or even eliminate a strategy to maintain that threshold instead of driving a lower rate.

Walt: There is another reason for our policy. If your effective rate is too low on that much income, it could be a red flag for the IRS. The IRS can find unusual items in your tax return you may not have realized. For example, many of our clients have farms, and before they approached us, they took rather extravagant deductions. In other cases, when the IRS audited, they found something in one tax year, and then they opened another tax year and another. Suddenly, those clients had a mess. So, you want to do everything you can to keep an audit at bay.

Todd: You certainly do not want an audit by taking unnecessary risks. Studies conducted in the last decade by the Congressional Budget Office expect taxpayers to be in the 15-17% range when doing their own budgeting. That is a litmus test for us. We could legally reduce some of our clients' tax burdens all the way to zero, but we feel not only is there a moral obligation to pay taxes, but there is also a practical reason as well: you want to avoid drawing the attention of the IRS by making $500,000 and not paying a dime in taxes.

Develop a plan to make you a smaller target for the IRS. This is especially true when there is a lot of income to protect. Quite simply, one way is how items are presented on the return. Another way is applying tax code rules and regulations we have learned are beneficial to our clients. No one knows the exact mechanism the IRS uses to pull the returns for an audit, but if there is a vast discrepancy between the gross and net numbers, that can be a concern. Therefore, we do not recommend seeking every last tax dollar in savings. An audit is a lengthy hassle, and you want to avoid it if possible.

Walt: In this book, we will outline techniques you can use to

NUMBER OF AMERICANS BY TAX BRACKET

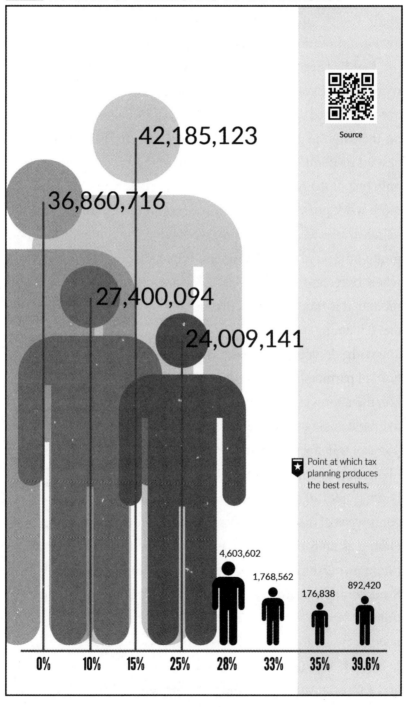

Source

42,185,123

36,860,716

27,400,094

24,009,141

Point at which tax planning produces the best results.

4,603,602

1,768,562

176,838

892,420

| 0% | 10% | 15% | 25% | 28% | 33% | 35% | 39.6% |

accomplish your goal. We mentioned earlier that the techniques we will discuss would work best if you are self-employed. You might wonder if the concepts in this book can be applied if you own a corporation or are part of a partnership.

Todd: These techniques can work for partnerships, but it works best if your partnership has fewer than seven partners. In our experience, it becomes challenging to coordinate everyone on the same page when you are dealing with particularly successful professionals. Part of our planning process will work if only one of the partners decides to engage it. Nonetheless, much more work goes on to make it successful than if all the individuals participate. For example, we have clients in an orthopedic group of around fifteen partners. We made our techniques work when only half of those partners are our clients. Ultimately, though, it is much easier if everyone collaborates.

Walt: If you participate in a normal partnership, and if you attain the approval of your partners to operate using these techniques, you can transfer your partnership ownership to another entity. That is a key part of making the concepts we will discuss in this book work. However, if you are operating as an S corporation, it is important to know an S corporation ownership cannot be held in any entity. You can only own S corporation shares as an individual. That means you cannot transfer your ownership interest into an entity, which you will need to create for many of these concepts to work.

> ## "YOU SHOULD HAVE A GOAL OF REDUCING YOUR EFFECTIVE TAX RATE TO AROUND 15 PERCENT."
>
> WALT DALLAS

Todd: Whether you are a sole proprietor, an S corporation, an LLC, or a partnership, the planning we will discuss will have a certain impact on your business.

Many of our clients started their own businesses and broke away from a secure job to go into business for themselves. Numerous people, including their spouses, probably thought they were making a huge mistake by taking on the liability and risk, giving up a steady paycheck, and working nine to five. Our clients seem to encompass an entrepreneurial spirit. Many possess Type-A personalities and know there is more to the Tax Code than what they have been given. Our clients can make decisions for themselves without asking permission.

> "OUR CLIENTS SEEM TO HAVE THAT ENTREPRENEURIAL SPIRIT. MANY HAVE TYPE-A PERSONALITIES AND KNOW THERE'S MORE TO THE TAX CODE THAN WHAT THEY'VE BEEN GIVEN."
>
> TODD MARDIS

Walt: That's part of maintaining control of your income. Not only do you need the ability to direct where the money goes, but you also need to be decisive about it. Our clients want to control the environment and do it their way because they think it will be superior to their competition. As part of our annual review process, they look at how their gross and net income is growing and how their employees' expenses relate on a percentage basis. They evaluate a detailed and written marketing plan specific to their business. In the annual review process, when clients are engaged in the planning, they are receiving mitigation of income taxes and see the top line escalate. Todd excels at coaching business owners on how to increase their revenue consistently. If they are like most of our clients and follow the planning we are conducting in our annual meetings, they will see their revenue and profits increase.

Todd: Individuals who understand their business and how it is structured, who understand basic accounting principles such as gross revenue, taxable income, depreciation, and general expenses, are much better at adapting to our plans.

Walt: The more involved our clients are in their business financial issues, the better they understand what we are working towards and how it fits together. Many times for the first time, our clients become proactive. They understand how our structures work and can add unique items to their particular situation. We work with a group of entrepreneurial-type orthodontists. They are excellent clients because they understand the ins and outs of their business and the plan's structure.

> "OUR CLIENTS TEND TO BE THE ENTREPRENURIAL TYPE THAT WANT TO RUN THEIR OWN PLACE."
>
> WALT DALLAS

Sometimes, other groups are not as engaged in structural aspects. Orthopedic surgeons may struggle because they often focus so many hours on practicing medicine instead of managing the business end of their practice. It can be difficult to arrange and explain a complex plan to people who are not immersed in the business world every day.

Todd: We also work with business owners who exclusively receive a paycheck. These individuals usually maintain a back office that keeps track of their accounts receivables and an eye on expenses. We can still help business owners in that position, but there is a learning curve for those who do not sustain day-to-day contact with payroll, benefits, and other general expenses. This is typically due to the time constraints in their profession. We create separate structures for those clients and flow their income to this new structure from a general partnership. This, many times, provides immediate tax relief. Instead of flowing to the individual, the income flows to an S corporation with a separate federal tax ID number.

Walt: If you are at the end of the spectrum and spend less time running your business than practicing your craft, this book can still help you. Nonetheless, you should expect to spend extra time developing an understanding of these tax planning measures' structural aspects.

Todd: There is one other kind of person who will find this book useful. If you desired to reduce your taxes but did not know where to turn, these techniques are for you. Many of our clients knew they needed to reduce their taxes, but they did not understand how. Ultimately, they fell back into the rat race of funding the 401(k) and spending a dollar to save forty cents.

DO YOU CONTROL YOUR INCOME SOURCE? A REQUIREMENT FOR ADVANCED TAX PLANNING

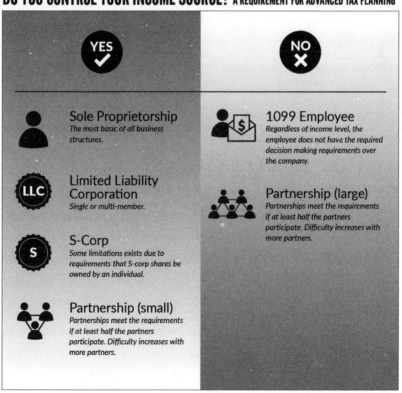

YES ✓

Sole Proprietorship
The most basic of all business structures.

Limited Liability Corporation
Single or multi-member.

S-Corp
Some limitations exists due to requirements that S-corp shares be owned by an individual.

Partnership (small)
Partnerships meet the requirements if at least half the partners participate. Difficulty increases with more partners.

NO ✗

1099 Employee
Regardless of income level, the employee does not have the required decision making requirements over the company.

Partnership (large)
Partnerships meet the requirements if at least half the partners participate. Difficulty increases with more partners.

A client in California did a great job of suppressing his taxes, but it cost him a lot of money. He invested in solar panels, swapped over to energy-efficient windows, and took advantage of just about every tax credit he could find on a federal and state level. When he was referred to us, the first comment he made was, "I'm tired of spending money to reduce my taxes." We hear that a lot. People want to reduce their taxes, and they know people who have a successful plan. They start researching, which is great, but the recommendations they receive are to purchase a piece of property, fund a 401(k), or add a profit-sharing plan. There is nothing inherently wrong with any of those strategies, as those options certainly provide tax deductions and temporary tax relief. Nevertheless, you should ask yourself if you really need or even want a particular tax deduction. Think about our California client who was weary of spending more money to save on his taxes. The truth is the Tax Codes provide much more effective and efficient strategies.

Not only can we help you save taxes without spending so much, but these strategies will also help no matter where you live. We have clients in just about every state in the union, from coast to coast, north to south. Our planning works in all fifty states, and it performs even better in states with high income taxes like California and New York. When we work with clients in states who enjoy zero state income tax, such as Alaska, Florida, Nevada, South Carolina, Texas, Washington, and Wyoming, it is imperative to generate enough savings on the federal side for the plan to make sense.

> "OUR PLANNING WORKS IN ALL FIFTY STATES, AND IT PERFORMS EVEN BETTER IN STATES THAT HAVE HIGH INCOME TAXES LIKE CALIFORNIA AND NEW YORK."
>
> TODD MARDIS

Walt: Bottom line, the planning will work no matter where you live. If you obtain enough income and control, these techniques will help you. If you live somewhere that does not charge state taxes, your plan might look different. Nonetheless, you can still use our strategies.

Todd: If you meet the criteria we discussed, you are ready to start learning how to save money. We will start with a subject that can scare even the most experienced businessperson - let's discuss the Internal Revenue Code.

KEY TAKEAWAYS

- Your goal should NOT be to pay zero taxes. This both undermines the legitimate needs of our society and increases your risk of audit.

- While tax planning can benefit most every American, the greatest benefit is recognized when your income level exceeds approximately $350,000.

- To take advantage of the most productive tax planning vehicles, you must have the ability to control the source of your income (i.e. from an LLC, S Corporation, or Partnership, as opposed to being a W2 employee).

- The individuals who are most successful at tax planning are those that have an entrepreneurial spirit, and are accustomed to giving a great deal of attention to working *on* their business rather than working *in* their business.

VIDEO RESOURCES

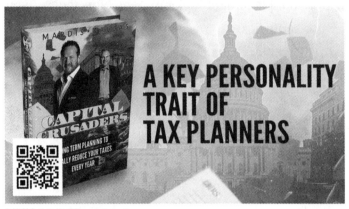

LINK: bit.ly/Crusaders1

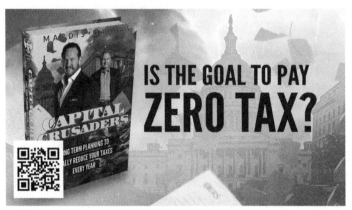

LINK: bit.ly/Crusaders2

ALBERT EINSTEIN

"THE HARDEST THING IN
THE WORLD TO UNDERSTAND
IS THE INCOME TAX."

Run to the tax code

Walt: Your planning strategy should always start with the United States Tax Code. We know it can be daunting, but that is where all the tax savings are.

Todd: Many of our clients and their advisors were afraid of the Tax Code when they started with us. If their CPAs were not engaging in strategies and structures available in the Tax Code, the clients had very few options outside of funding their 401(k) plans or buying something in December to reduce their taxes. That kind of thinking baffles us. I can assure you the Mitt Romneys and Warren Buffets of the world are not waiting until December to purchase items hoping to save money. They are not investing $55,000 in a 401(k). Those two strategies alone cannot drive their tax liability to the desired rate of 17%.

Walt: Many of the CPAs with whom we have worked with do not even read the Tax Code.

Todd: Unfortunately, that is true. We were in a meeting with a CPA who was approaching retirement, so he had been practicing for some time. We quoted and summarized several sections of the Tax Code. The CPA responded by saying, "I don't read tax codes." We were absolutely stunned. This was an experienced CPA who was responsible for managing his client's taxes. We could not believe he would admit, especially in front of his client, that he never read the laws he was trying to help his clients abide by.

Walt: The Tax Code can be rather intimidating, though. If you were to turn the Internal Revenue Code into a standard-sized book, it would be about ten inches thick, even in tiny print. When you add all the regulations, that's about another fifty books.

> "I THINK IT'S SAFE TO SAY NOBODY KNOWS THE ENTIRE CODE."
>
> WALT DALLAS

Todd: The U. S. Master Tax Guide is 1,000 pages and merely includes the definitions. Furthermore, it is written in a font you need a microscope to read!

Walt: I think it is safe to say no one knows the entire code. Some people know how to work in a particular section, but no one could be an expert with the entire Code.

Todd: The fundamental problem with not reading the Tax Code is that everything you can do as a business owner to save taxes is outlined in black and white. Ninety percent of the U.S. Masters Tax Guide is a dedicated blueprint to guide a business owner on deducting certain liabilities and expenses. The Tax

GROWING FEDERAL TAX LAW IN PAGE LENGTH

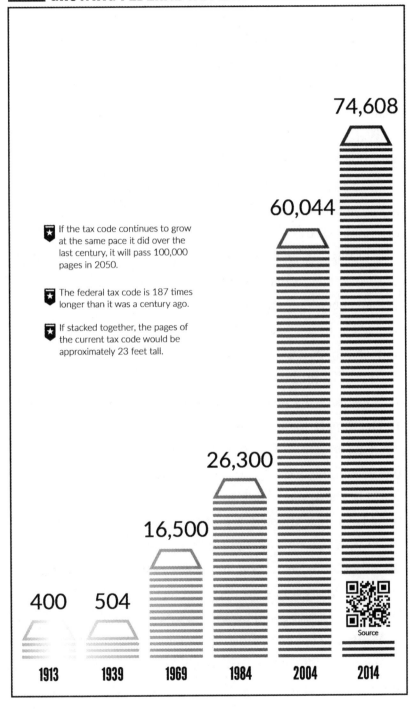

If the tax code continues to grow at the same pace it did over the last century, it will pass 100,000 pages in 2050.

The federal tax code is 187 times longer than it was a century ago.

If stacked together, the pages of the current tax code would be approximately 23 feet tall.

74,608

60,044

26,300

16,500

400   504

Source

1913   1939   1969   1984   2004   2014

Code is a mechanism by which a business owner understands what they can and cannot deduct, given different structures and scenarios.

Walt: That is precisely why we say, "Run to the Tax Code."

Todd: Run to the Code, learn what is available to you, safely utilize it, and follow the Code's intent.

Walt: The magic is combining different code sections into a cohesive plan. Anyone can pick a section and find a deduction. The real value is how you take those code provisions and formulate a plan to fit your situation. If you back up everything you do with a provision from the Tax Code, there is a built-in argument if you are ever audited. Everything in our planning process has a tax code section behind it.

> ## "THE MAGIC IS IN PUTTING DIFFERENT CODE SECTIONS TOGETHER INTO A COHESIVE PLAN."
>
> WALT DALLAS

Todd: To further understand tax codes, consider this: Congress intentionally enacted tax laws to provide business owners with legitimate and useful deductions. In many cases, legislators pass laws because of lobbyists. Most senators and representatives have lobbyists in their ear the entire time they are in session. They are paid to talk to Congress about things they want in the laws. Ask yourself, who are they typically lobbying for? Wealthy people, right? People with money are the only ones who can afford lobbyists. If you do not have money, you cannot hire a lobbyist. Many times, we see code sections more applicable to those who are successful business owners.

Walt: The big companies know how to play the game. They are funding lobbyists to provide tax breaks many times to certain industries and sectors. However, the good thing about the

Tax Code is big businesses and wealthy people are not the only groups who can take advantage of the tax breaks once they are passed. These tax breaks are available for small businesses as well. Let's face it: it's impossible to write a tax law and have it only applied to a large corporation. Ultimately, these tax codes are available to everyone. Keep that in mind when you read the Tax Code. Determine deductions that were passed for large businesses, but everyone should be using.

One of our favorite tax codes is Section 831(b), which allows you to create a private insurance company. A business that owns its own insurance company will insure against a controlled risk and diligently ensure those risks do not turn into claims. When a business pays premiums to a commercial carrier, it has a deduction. When it pays premiums to its own private insurance company, it also takes a deduction. The Code allows you to own your insurance company, receive the benefits of good loss control and fewer claims, and retain tax-deductible premiums.

Todd: For instance, let's say you are a civil engineer who builds bridges. There is a risk that you could be sued if the abutments are installed improperly, or there is a miscalculation of materials, which leads to a collapse. There are several ways to manage this risk. You could purchase errors and omissions insurance, or you can pay premiums to your own private insurance company to cover the mistake and to rebuild the bridge. The Tax Code allows you to insure or retain risk if it is priced actuarially by a third party. When you retain the risk, if you do not pay out a claim, the premiums your company has made are also retained as profits or excess premiums and are tax-deductible. The question becomes, would you rather pay an outside insurance company to potentially cover claims, or pay premiums to your own insurance company and keep the funds in the event you never have a claim?

A real-life example of utilizing this tax code is United Parcel Service. UPS formed their own insurance company to cover the risk of lost or damaged packages. If they were to lose a package with a $2,000 value, they could file a claim against their own insurance company. If they do not lose or damage a package, they will retain the premiums spent on their private insurance company. In 2001, the IRS filed a case against UPS on the premise that there was no need for them to have their own insurance company as UPS rarely lost or damaged packages.

Walt: The question was whether you could have an insurance company with no claims. The IRS was probably looking back three years since that is the statute of limitations. I am sure UPS has had claims for loss, but they likely found a three-year period where there were very few, or possibly even no claims at all. Therefore, the IRS challenged them on it. UPS argued it was still a real risk. It is a risk they manage well, but it is still a risk. Ultimately, UPS won because it was in the Code—the Code does not require an insurance company to have claims. It was a landmark case.

Todd: The regulations do not really define insurance. The Supreme Court held that insurance requires risk shifting and distribution. If the contract shifts and distributes a risk of loss, it counts as insurance if the risk is insurable. Plus, that kind of risk management works for more than just errors and omissions.

For example, you can insure the loss of a key employee. Let's say there are two architects who design high rise buildings, and they each have a staff built around working with both of them. If one of them becomes disabled or dies, there would be a loss of revenue and continued overhead costs. Their company could own a key employee agreement and file a claim to cover the lost revenue the partner generated, cover all the other employees' costs allocated to the disabled architect, and allow time to hire a new architect.

Walt: A client, who is an attorney, was engaging in a lot of real estate closings. He routinely kept a couple of million dollars in his escrow account and was worried about internal theft. He had ten employees, and he was concerned that if one of them figured out a way to steal from him, he could be out two million dollars. He could not find insurance for that need, so we helped him set up a private insurance company. Now, the client is making tax-deductible premium payments to his own insurance company. Assuming he can keep his claim rates low, he will benefit from the company.

Todd: Another client wanted to insure against the loss of a key customer. This individual lives in the Midwest and provides a particular item to the Subway restaurant chains. You can imagine what would happen to his business if he lost his contract with Subway. He would have a lot of product on his hands and nothing to do with it. He set up a reserve to keep him afloat in the event he lost the contract with Subway and needed time to find another company.

> ## "IF YOU WANT TO REDUCE YOUR TAX LIABILITY, YOU HAVE TO START YOUR PLANNING WITH THE CODE."
>
> WALT DALLAS

Walt: The point is, the Tax Code provides all kinds of created scenarios specifically to help businesses save money on taxes. If you want to reduce your tax liability, you must start your planning using the Code.

Todd: Developing your plan by "running to the Tax Code" is imperative *before* events happen and when it is time to file your returns. By the time you are ready to file your returns, you look at past scenarios. This form of planning is reactive and can be detrimental to your financial future. It is crucial to be *proactive* and stay in front of possible tax liabilities.

Walt: This is especially true considering how technology has evolved. Now, all the provisions in the Code are entered into these wonderful computer programs. This means your tax preparation is nothing but data entry. Many times, when a person approaches their CPA with a tax question, the CPA will enter the data into their system and let the software program answer for them. Your tax preparer enters the numbers in the right field and presses a button to determine what you owe in taxes. There are very few advisors reading the Code who utilize its content effectively. The problem is the software is reactive; it does not allow for proactive planning. Proactive planning is knowing how to structure your finances and then position the right pieces in place to take the Code's deductions. The software is a great tool, but you cannot let it do all the work. You must run to the Code and develop a plan you can set into action.

Todd: A client of ours approached us with a situation that illustrates this point. He owned a second home in the mountains. Essentially, he owned an expensive asset/liability. He paid maintenance fees, property taxes, and utilities. At the end of the year, he discovered he could take a depreciation deduction if he had tried to rent out the property. He had not rented the home, but he took an invalid deduction on his return. He was audited and hit with interest and penalties in ad-

> "THIS KIND OF PLANNING TAKES A LOT OF STUDYING AND A LOT OF WORK, SO DON'T TRY TO RUSH IT. IT WON'T HAPPEN OVERNIGHT."
>
> TODD MARDIS

dition to the tax. I asked him if he had engaged in any planning to attempt to rent the property. I asked him, "Do you have an agreement with a realtor? Do you actually have any rentals? Did you take any action to show you were in the business of renting the property?" He had not, and he simply filed the returns. This is not the way you run to the Code. The way you run to the Code is to find out the rules, follow the rules, and then take the deduction. Think about it this way: if I were to tell Walt to compete in the Olympics, his obvious question would be, "What event?" If I could not tell him, he would not properly train, nor would he know the rules. When you show up at the end of the year and tell your CPA to save you as much as they can on your taxes, it is just like training for an athletic event. If you want to reduce your tax liability, you must plan and prepare in advance.

Walt: We cannot stress planning enough. Understand, developing and implementing the plan will take some time. We have a process to design the plan, create the structure, and then roll it out to the client over 3-5 months. We start by explaining their customized plan to understand the overall design and how the pieces fit together. Then we have a series of meetings to walk them through the documentation process and expectations. At this time, the CPA prepares the tax returns based upon the records we create.

Todd: Implementing a proper plan does not happen overnight. It is vitally important to take adequate time to understand and maximize the benefits of the plan.

Walt: Now that you know how to begin tax planning, you are probably ready to dive in and find deductions. Before you do, there are a few other things you need to consider. In the next chapter, we will discuss the changing tax rates and why it matters as we design your customized plan.

② KEY TAKEAWAYS

Though daunting due to its length, the United States tax code is the blueprint for how to save money on your taxes. It contains all rules and instructions for how to legally pay lower taxes. Embrace this fact and dive in!

Tax laws are greatly impacted by lobbyists hired by big corporations and wealthy individuals. However, while the laws may have been passed due to the efforts of the mega-wealthy, the resulting laws can be utilized and taken advantage by every American.

The Tax Code is most beneficial when it is used as a tool to proactively plan your future tax strategy, as opposed to using it in an attempt to find last minute savings.

▶ VIDEO RESOURCES

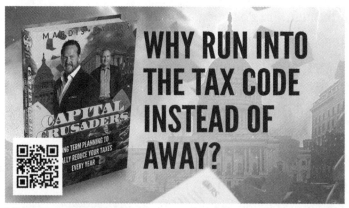

LINK: bit.ly/Crusaders3

PRESIDENT GEORGE H.W. BUSH

"READ MY LIPS:
NO NEW TAXES!"

ARE TAXES GOING UP OR DOWN?

Walt: No discussion about tax planning would be complete without examining tax rates. You must take them into account when you are developing tax savings strategies.

Todd: Keep in mind, the current landscape is positioning us for significant tax increases.

Walt: To some extent, tax rates are related to which political party controls the government. As you know, recent trends make it easy to determine which direction tax rates are moving. Right now, in 2021, we are at a historical low in marginal tax brackets of 37%. When I was in college, the Maxi Tax was imposed. The tax rates were so high there had to be a maximum tax applied to your total earnings. Considering the current economic climate, it is likely we will see something similar again.

You see, when Obama was president, you had a standoff between the President and Congress. Obama looked at the George W. Bush tax cuts, and he had to decide whether he wanted to endorse them or not. He let them expire without taking any action, and the top marginal rate returned to 39.6%, where it was during the Clinton years. We are in that situation now, except the players are different. The Senate, House, and White House are all controlled by Democrats. Any legislation must have the approval of the House of Representatives to go forward. Trump implemented tax breaks under the 2017 Tax Cuts and Job Act (TCJA), but without the House approval, those tax breaks would sunset the way they did during the Obama years. We could be looking at the same 39.6% top federal rate once again. Because of that phase-out, taxes could very well increase.

> **"THERE ARE BETWEEN 35-40 PERCENT OF THE POPULATION TODAY THAT DO NOT PAY TAXES AT ALL."**
>
> TODD MARDIS

Nonetheless, there is an even more pressing issue. There is an immense amount of government spending right now. Our political leanings seem to be to the left, which is more toward socialism than capitalism. Candidates made promises of free tuition, free health care, and student loan forgiveness. Somehow, we must pay for those programs. Unless they raise taxes to pay for government obligations, rapid inflation is inevitable.

Todd: Statistically speaking, those individuals earning over $200,000 pay 58.9% of all taxes paid in the U.S. People who earn between $100,000 and $200,000 pay 21% of the taxes. There are between 35-40% of the total population today who do not pay taxes at all.

HISTORICAL MARGINAL TAX RATES LOWEST TO HIGHEST BRACKETS

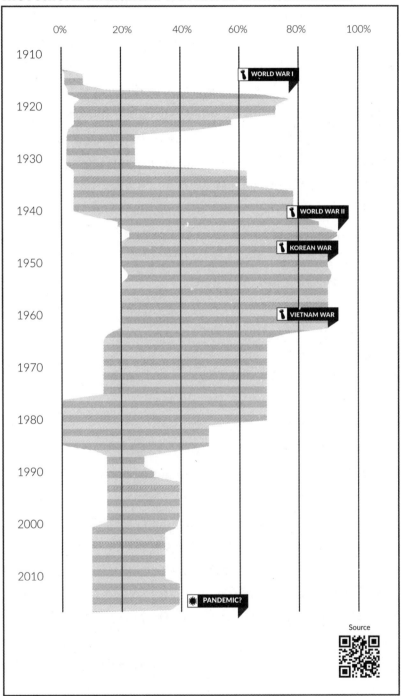

Walt: Here is another interesting statistic: the bottom half of taxpayers in this country are earning $40,000 a year or less and paying about 3% in taxes.

Todd: In essence, fewer people are being taxed, and more money needs to be raised. Individuals who earn over $200,000 will likely see their tax rates increase dramatically. If Congress does not jump on board to reduce spending, not only will the deficit continue to increase, but taxes will increase as well. Both political parties tend to overspend, so it really does not matter which party controls the government. If they do not control spending and the deficit keeps growing, there must be resources to cover them.

Walt: During the Carter years, the top marginal rates were 70%. Then Reagan came in with significant tax cuts. He dropped them down below 30%. The rates increased during the Clinton years, then George W. Bush lowered the rate to 30%. As we mentioned, Obama allowed those cuts to expire, which caused them to jump back up to 39.6%. So, there is a pattern. Rates increase, someone comes in with one broad stroke to lower them, and inevitably they creep up again.

> "THERE ARE CERTAIN PEOPLE IN WASHINGTON LOOKING AT ALL OF THAT MONEY THAT'S SITTING IN YOUR QUALIFIED RETIREMENT ACCOUNTS AND VIEWING IT AS MONEY THEY CAN SPEND."
>
> WALT DALLAS

Todd: There is a history of volatile tax rates, and it is fascinating when you research the first part of the twentieth century. During World War I, the top rates soared after being less than 10% during Wilson's first term. They dropped substantially during the 1920s, and then the top marginal rate increased to 63% during the Great Depression. The top marginal rate steadily increased until it reached 94% in 1944. The top rate would stay at 91% through the Eisenhower years. In fact, it stayed above 90% for twenty years, until 1964.

Walt: When I was in accounting school, one of my professors explained how his clients could have paid more than 100% on what they earned in 1978. This was during the Carter years when the top federal rate alone was 70%.

Todd: Reagan made such a huge impact by dropping the rate by around 40%. During the first year of his presidency, federal income tax rates were lowered significantly with the signing of the Economic Recovery Tax Act of 1981, which lowered the top marginal tax bracket from 70% to 50%.

The point is, once rates began to increase, it took fifty years to reduce them again. While the more recent ups and downs of the top marginal tax rates are not nearly as dramatic as what individuals went through 75-100 years ago, we are deeply divided as a country and in the midst of a very volatile political era. There is just no way to know who will be in power five, ten, and fifteen years from now—and what those in Washington will do regarding our tax rates. The real question is, what will they be forced to do?

Walt: For the foreseeable future, we think we should plan on rates increasing. It does not matter who is in control. A simple look at our country's financial obligations tells you that there will be insufficient funds to pay them if we do not trim those social budgets.

Todd: The federal deficit for 2020 is $3.3 trillion. We collected $3.42 trillion in revenue, and we spent $6.6 trillion. Consequently, we spent roughly $3 trillion more than we collected. Fifth-grade math tells you it does not work for very long. Eventually, our country will be forced to remedy the problem. Today's borrowing is largely appropriate and necessary to reduce and distribute over time the economic pain caused by the COVID-19 pandemic. But the CBO's newest figures show our long-term course is unsustainable and much worse than before. Once the current crisis ends, policymakers must turn their attention to long-term deficit reduction to set the country on solid fiscal ground.

Walt: Both the House and Senate agree our budgetary deficit is much too high, and we will see action soon if everyone in Washington agrees.

Todd: The way you remedy the problem is to cut spending, which Congress has refused to do, or bring in more money. It does not take much insight to look at the political landscape and figure out what will happen.

Walt: Legislative action on taxes usually takes place in an incoming president's first year. We should see tax increases in early 2021. Nothing is certain in the political arena, but that is a pretty good guess.

Todd: We truly believe taxes will increase over the next 10-20 years. The amount in which taxes increase will largely be dependent on who the majority is in Congress, but either way,

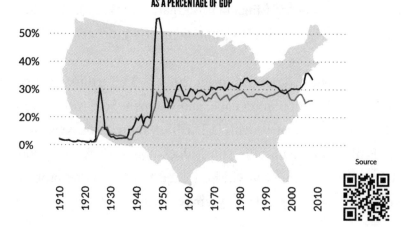

FEDERAL RECEIPTS VS EXPENDITURES
AS A PERCENTAGE OF GDP

Source

you will see increases.

Walt: Unfortunately, taxes are not the only way to address the deficit problem. Right now, many in Congress are looking for a pile of money, and they think they found it. There has been legislation proposed to borrow money from qualified retirement plans. There are certain people in Washington looking at all the money sitting in your qualified retirement accounts and viewing it as the money they can spend.

Todd: The idea is the government will borrow your money from your 401(k) and then pay you a stated interest rate. An article on retirement assets published by the Investment Company Institute stated as of September 30, 2019, there was $5.9 trillion in assets, which consists of 19% of the $30.1 trillion total in those retirement accounts. That is a tremendous amount of money sitting on the sidelines in these plans, and Congress has proposed using it to cover government programs and expenses. One question is whether the political landscape has moved so far to the left they would use that $30.1 trillion as social capital.

Walt: In addition to looking at the IRAs as social capital, there used to be a 15% extra tax on your IRA on excess accumulations. Imagine if the government encouraged people to save as much as they could for retirement plans, then suddenly they decided to hit them with an additional 15% tax on what they deemed "excess savings." Ultimately, it was repealed. Still, it has been in the Code before.

Todd: The SECURE Act also changed the rules connected to inherited IRAs. They fast-forwarded the timing of distributions you must take, which means more taxes sooner.

Walt: That was a huge surprise. Historically, you could stretch those inherited IRAs over your lifetime instead of paying a lump sum tax on them. Nowadays, if you inherit an IRA from a parent, you must pay the tax within five years. When the taxes are due on qualified retirement plans, there may be a similar issue. Keep in mind there is a lot of money in IRAs. When money is distributed, it will be subject to a tax rate determined by Congress in the future. All Congress needs to do to generate taxes on those plans is change when the money is paid to you. So, if your life savings are in a qualified retirement plan, you should come to terms with the fact Congress can make adjustments that can significantly impact your retirement income and lifestyle.

Todd: Do you still have faith in your qualified plan? You see, it is not just about your income or fluctuating taxes. We should consider all the other ways the good people in Washington have not figured out how to tax American citizens.

Walt: The bottom line is there are two things to be concerned about. The first is short-term tax planning year by year and dropping your marginal rate on your income, which is our forte. Secondly, you also need to be concerned about long-term tax planning. Are you creating a tax planning problem down the road? If you accumulate high balances in your qualified retirement plans, you will need to pay taxes on those funds at the highest marginal rate, whatever that is, when you withdraw them. Consider the long-term implications of your plan. How can you accumulate wealth with as little tax burden as possible? As rates creep higher, the planning you do now will most likely have an exponentially greater value to you and your family.

Todd: As an investor, you should be concerned about how much you earn *and* ultimately **keep**. When you consider the ever-changing tax rates, the government's control over your current income, and what is set aside for retirement, planning becomes imperative to financial survival.

Walt: Knowing taxes are likely to increase, tax planning becomes even more crucial. An aspect of tax planning that is every bit as important as developing the best strategy to save tax dollars and provide for your future is audit protection. As you turn our advice into your own tax strategy, you will want to include our tips for reducing your audit risk and successfully defending an audit. We will start in the next chapter with an overview of how the audit process works.

③ KEY TAKEAWAYS

- We are in a historically low period for income tax rates. Coupled with continued government spending, it is a virtual certainty that taxes will increase.

- Income taxes are just one way the federal government can access your money. Americans currently have $30 trillion sitting in retirement savings accounts, and many government officials are looking at ways to access that money as well.

- Your tax strategy should contain both short-term mechanisms for lowering your marginal rate, and long-term mechanisms that allow you to accumulate money without having to pay maximum taxes on it in the future.

▶ VIDEO RESOURCES

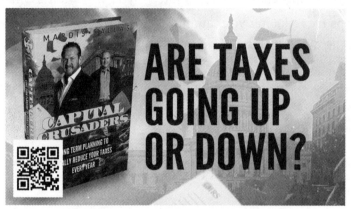

LINK: bit.ly/Crusaders4

MARK TWAIN

"I SHALL NEVER USE PROFANITY
EXCEPT IN DISCUSSING HOUSE RENT
AND TAXES."

WHAT IS AN AUDIT DEFENSE PLAN?

Walt: We recognize being audited is a common fear when implementing tax strategies. Audits can be a complex system. Understanding how the system works makes developing your documentation and substantiation or justifying your deduction much easier.

Todd: Many people think audits are a big, scary ordeal. They believe IRS agents are two-headed, red-eyed monsters, and that really is not the case. They are individuals who have jobs, just like you and me. The job of the IRS auditor is to ensure you are complying with the Tax Code. That is all there is to it. The biggest problem we have seen with audits is consistency. Most auditors are extremely astute and understand the big picture. Others have trouble wrapping their heads around it, so they simply deny everything. In those cases, the trick is to explain everything in an organized way so the auditors can understand the plan you are attempting to implement. Once they understand what you are trying to do, they are more likely to accept this kind of planning.

Some of these techniques are things a few IRS auditors have never seen before, plain and simple. An auditor once told me, "I've just never seen that before." That answer is a great one for us. We want them to come at us with "You can't do it because I've never seen that," because we can show them that you can.

> **"THAT'S LITERALLY A QUOTE I HEARD FROM AN AUDITOR ONCE: *'I'VE JUST NEVER SEEN THAT BEFORE.'"***
>
> TODD MARDIS

As we describe the process, you will see that as it goes through different levels, there are a few opportunities to explain the strategies. In our experience, if we have our documentation and substantiation ready, the IRS allows the deduction.

The first question clients generally ask is, "Why am I being selected for an audit?" The IRS has a computer system known as the Discriminant Function System. They run all tax returns through this system, which looks for anomalies in the returns. They compare tax returns against "norms" for similar returns, and the system performs a test based on income and deductions. If the W-2's do not match up or there are errors in the return, the system will catch it and flag it for review. If the IRS selects a return for examination, it does not necessarily mean the taxpayer has either made a mistake or been dishonest. In fact, examinations can result in a refund or acceptance without change.

Flags for further examination can happen if income is underreported. Many times, people unintentionally underreport income. There might be a 1099 that comes out late and is not counted. Still, that is a red flag.

Of course, if someone is underreporting on purpose, that can set the stage for immense trouble. If they are in the midst of an audit and have intentionally avoided reporting income or intentionally taken deductions they knew they weren't supposed to, they should be afraid of an audit. The IRS will come down very hard, particularly for not reporting income. This is called tax evasion, and a taxpayer can end up in an orange jumpsuit if they do so. This does not mean we cannot create the most effective corporate structure to mitigate income tax. We just need to report the income in the first place.

Walt: This raises a good point. An effective corporate structure is important. If you do not have a corporate structure and are taking all your income on a Schedule C, this can also be an audit flag.

> "IF YOU DON'T HAVE A CORPORATE STRUCTURE AND YOU'RE TAKING ALL OF YOUR INCOME ON A SCHEDULE C, THAT CAN ALSO BE AN AUDIT FLAG."
>
> WALT DALLAS

Todd: Schedule C income from an LLC is a highly audited area. Your odds of becoming audited are around 2.4% if you file a Schedule C and earn between $25,000 and $100,000. Those odds increase if you take certain actions and deductions.

Walt: If the taxpayer keeps his business expenses on a Schedule C as part of the 1040 form and no entity, such as an S Corporation, is listed, the IRS may think there is improper reporting. Schedule C income, with no entity, represents a lower level of sophistication. The lowest bar to clear with the IRS and the easiest entity to form is an LLC, otherwise known as a limited liability company. The next step up would be the S Corporation or C Corporation. There are built-in checks and balances with those, and the owner needs a certain level of sophistication. Schedule C income creates a situation where mistakes can be made. If something arouses their suspicion, the light the IRS shines becomes that much brighter when a lot of income is in play.

Todd: That's fairly common. It's easy for the CPA to recommend setting up an LLC, and it's often the correct corporate structure at that time. When you launch a business, you probably need to file as an LLC. There are not many tax benefits if you do not have income stemming from an S Corporation, and there is also the expense of preparing and filing a corporate return. We often see business owners who started with an LLC and did very well over time, but they just never evolved from an LLC.

Walt: We also see many people in partnership LLCs, where an individual owns the partnership interest instead of an entity, creating Schedule C income.

Todd: In whatever way you end up with Schedule C income, what the IRS is looking for is people deducting non-business expenses.

Walt: They're looking for a lot of personal expenses being deducted as business expenses.

Todd: That's easy to correct. If we move the client into an S Corporation, we can avoid many payroll taxes they would normally pay. It is an easy planning fix; you receive tax benefits and reduce audit risk in one simple little play.

We will talk more about creating effective corporate structures in Chapter Twelve.

Walt: Another audit risk is "listed transactions." The IRS has determined certain types of transactions are tax scams. Anything on that list, things they know on the front end they disagree with, will catch their attention quicker.

Todd: Those types of transactions usually have substantial tax benefits. That does not necessarily mean they are wrong or illegal, but the IRS will want to look at it because they may have a problem with how you have filed your return. Examples of listed transactions are Offshore Deferred Compensation Arrangements, Partnership Straddle Tax Shelters, Basis Shifting Tax Shelters, and many more.

Walt: When you look at the number of people in lower-income brackets who receive random audits, those numbers are rather low until income drops below $25,000. Audit rates for wage earners under $25,000 are significantly higher than overall audit rates, but those audit rates drop when wages exceed $25,000 and stay low until income exceeds $500,000.

Todd: In fact, people with income between $100,000 and $200,000 typically have less than a .44% chance of being audited. That is about one out of 225 people at this income level. One of the biggest factors for many people becoming audited is their income level.

Walt: If you are making more than a million dollars, the rate increases. Taxpayers with an annual income above $10 million

BENEFITS OF AN AUDIT DEFENSE PLAN

DECREASE YOUR CHANCES OF BEING AUDITED

★ Identify and eliminates unsound strategies.

★ Properly lowers adjusted gross income to help avert the interest of the IRS.

INCREASE YOUR CHANCES OF WINNING AN AUDIT

★ Proper organization and documentation sets the tone with the IRS agent.

★ All strategies are soundly rooted and confirmed by the tax code.

have the highest audit rates of all groups. One of the main factors for someone becoming audited is their income being higher than it should have been. If you can lower your adjusted gross income, that will reduce your chances of becoming audited. Think about a bank robber. Why do they rob banks? Because that is where the money is. The IRS can audit someone who earns $30,000 a year, but there is only so much they will be able to recover. People who have income over a million a year have a lot more to go after. As part of your planning process, if you can reduce income to a lower tax bracket, you will not be as attractive of a target.

Constitutional arguments also catch their attention. For example, if a taxpayer argues the IRS does not have the authority to tax income or wipe out the deduction they claim, the IRS will take immediate action to investigate.

They really like landing on "clever cheaters" with both feet—they have said so. People think they can cheat the system by taking this wild stance no one ever agrees with. Inevitably, they will not get away with it.

That is why working with tax attorneys, people with Master of Science in Taxation degrees, and other seasoned professionals is critical. They will not entertain crazy things like "the IRS doesn't have the authority." Take your tax plan to a professional who really grasps the Code, and they will help safeguard your strategy if you are under the scrutiny of an audit.

Some of our clients hold rental property. We review it every year to ensure total rental income is under 10% of gross income. We find if it exceeds that amount, it tends to attract the auditor's attention—they've as much as said so.

If a taxpayer is selected for an audit, the IRS will notify you by mail. They will not initiate this process by phone, email, pigeon, or any other form of communication.

There will be a directive in the letter to call a specific person to confirm it has been received. The letter informs you the IRS will start the audit, along with general areas they will be covering. At that point, it is a good idea to have a tax planner involved so they can help communicate with the IRS. Even if you develop these techniques on your own, it is good to have a tax planner on your side, especially if you think you might be impatient with the auditors. When we deal with auditors, they are very nice for the most part. They have a job to do and generally do not have a personal axe to grind. If you cooperate and make it pleasant for everyone, it goes well. If you are combative, it does not go well at all. Having that buffer between you and the IRS can be a good idea.

Once you contact the IRS through certified mail or fax, they go through their process, review the information, and provide a report. The report spells out what they will agree to and deny. They will send you a bill for what they think you need to pay. That does not mean you have to pay it right then - you have an option to appeal.

The IRS will request specific documents such as legal papers, loan agreements, receipts, and so on. We have a legal team who works on audits as we are most familiar with the strategies we can explain. Furthermore, we do not want our clients wasting time in numerous meetings with the IRS. We acquire powers of attorney from our clients, and we speak to the IRS and provide the requested documents on our clients' behalf.

Normally, the IRS can request items from as far back as three years in an audit. If the IRS finds a substantial error in the returns, they may add additional years and look back as far as six years.

Todd: The length of an audit varies depending on the type of audit, the complexity of the issues, how quickly documents can be provided, scheduling meetings, and if you agree or disagree with the findings.

There have been situations where we have had to agree with the IRS. For instance, sometimes, our clients go beyond the scope of the plans we set up. We are not talking about illegal or unethical things, but sometimes clients go beyond what most would consider reasonable. In those situations, we absolutely agree with the IRS that our client does owe money or is not entitled to as much in the way of a requested deduction. We

> "THE FEDERAL GOVERNMENT HAS TO USE UP A LOT OF MONEY AND RESOURCES TO TRY CASES IN TAX COURT, SO THEY TRY TO AVOID IT IF THEY CAN."
>
> WALT DALLAS

certainly do not go into IRS negotiations to argue the client is always right. We will defend our clients with everything we have but being reasonable with the IRS is the way to build credibility and rapport with them.

Walt: If you disagree with the audit findings, you will ask the IRS to send a "thirty-day letter," meaning you have thirty days from the letter's date to appeal their decision. That begins the appellate phase. The clock is ticking on the thirty days from the letter's date, regardless of when you receive it. You may have substantially less than thirty days, but the IRS is flexible and will usually give you additional time if needed. That is especially true if it happens to be during your CPA's busy season. However, if you received a "Notice of Deficiency" by certified mail, the IRS cannot grant you additional time to submit supporting documentation.

The appeals division is an independent division of the IRS.

The appeals office can be a little more comfortable with the auditors because they frequently work with them.

Todd: Because appeals officers have more experience and more accounting background, there are better opportunities to settle at an appeals level.

Walt: The appeal is where most of the cases are settled. Therefore, you want to appeal if you have the Code provisions and the documents to back up your deduction and they deny it anyway. The appellate division is rarely willing to try a case in Tax Court. The federal government expends a lot of money and resources to try cases in Tax Court, so they work to avoid it if they can. In the early days of my practice, the appeals officers used to be called Santa Claus. An individual would be working with an auditor who would not give anything, and then suddenly, the appeals officer was ready to strike a deal.

When we go into appeals, it is all about substantiation. We certainly give the legal arguments, but we focus on providing the substantiation for our case and careful documentation of everything.

If you do not settle there, you have the option of progressing to Tax Court. This time you receive a ninety-day letter, and you respond with a petition within the three-month window. There are no extensions granted in Tax Court. You must work within the ninety-day period from that letter. It is important to file your petition as soon as possible, using the United States Postal Service with a tracking number, and then follow up and ensure they document it by the letter's date. You may track your letter through their website at usps.com. If there is a problem, you have time to correct it. Disasters happen when you wait too long.

Todd: Most tax court cases will settle before you enter a courtroom. Judges at that level are very insistent upon parties

PHASES OF AN IRS AUDIT

IRS Notice Letter
The IRS will inform you of their intent to conduct an audit via a certified letter. The letter will detail the specific items and time periods they wish to audit. Now is the time to consider getting a tax planning professional involved to help manage the process.

IRS Report
This report will explain what deductions and transactions the IRS will allow and which they will deny. The report will also present a total amount the IRS believes you owe. You may choose to pay the amount or appeal.

30-Day Letter
If you chose to appeal, a request is made for a "30-Day Letter" which means you have thirty days from the date of the letter to make your formal appeal.

Appeal
Approximately 90% of cases are settled on appeal. The IRS agents at this level are typically more sophisticated and more familiar with the tax code than local auditors. The agents are very careful about proceeding to Tax Court as this requires a large investment of government resources.

90-Day Letter
If your case is not settled in the appeals phase, a "90-Day Letter" is issued. You MUST respond with your petition within the ninety-day period as no further extensions are granted.

Tax Court
Judges are insistent that parties work to settle before entering court. At this point you do have a bit of strategic advantage as you (and your attorney and/or CPA) have a much better understanding of your case than the tax attorney representing the IRS.

working together to settle the cases. You should be very well prepared by then if you go that far because you have already been through the audit and the appeals process. At that point, you have done your homework. However, the IRS attorney on the case will have seen it for the first time. Therefore, you will have a very high level of knowledge of the case, whereas the IRS attorney may not. In fact, they do not typically begin looking at the cases until a short time before they are heard. That, in turn, gives you a strategic opportunity to settle those cases right at the door of the Tax Court. You can take advantage of the IRS legal team not being quite as prepared as you are.

> "THERE ARE SEVERAL CONSIDERATIONS THAT GO INTO HOW MUCH OF A FIGHT YOU WANT TO PUT UP OVER AN AUDIT. THE AMOUNT OF MONEY AT STAKE IS ONE. ANOTHER IS HOW SOLID YOUR POSITION IS."
>
> TODD MARDIS

Walt: We worked with an auditor who drastically reduced our client's deduction. We felt the appeals officers were wrong, so we decided to take our chances in Tax Court. Within three days, an IRS attorney called and asked us to send them an offer. He further added they were ready to give our client 100% of the deduction (we had turned them down just days before when they offered 10% of the deduction). They were definitely trying to entice us in the subsequent phone call: "Let's settle this now. It will cost you money to go to court, and it will cost the federal government money." The government simply did not want to tie up their resources in Tax Court.

Todd: That's an important point. If you are an IRS auditor, and you are expending the resources of the federal government, would you rather go against a company that might have hundreds of thousands, or even millions, in back taxes, or an individual who might owe $15,000? Sometimes we might be willing

ODDS OF BEING AUDITED BY THE IRS BASED ON ADJUSTED GROSS INCOME

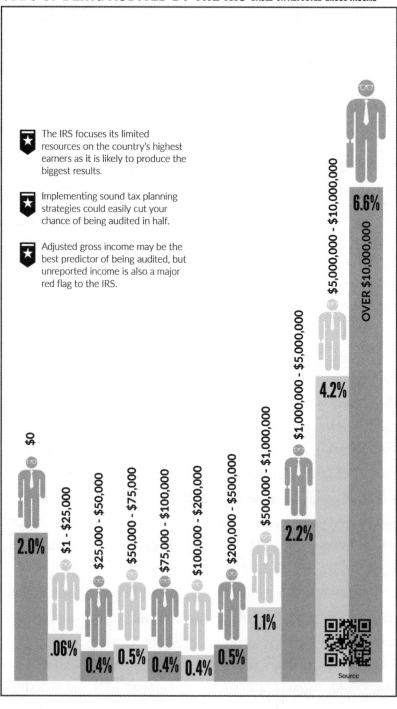

The IRS focuses its limited resources on the country's highest earners as it is likely to produce the biggest results.

Implementing sound tax planning strategies could easily cut your chance of being audited in half.

Adjusted gross income may be the best predictor of being audited, but unreported income is also a major red flag to the IRS.

$0 — 2.0%

$1 - $25,000 — .06%

$25,000 - $50,000 — 0.4%

$50,000 - $75,000 — 0.5%

$75,000 - $100,000 — 0.4%

$100,000 - $200,000 — 0.4%

$200,000 - $500,000 — 0.5%

$500,000 - $1,000,000 — 1.1%

$1,000,000 - $5,000,000 — 2.2%

$5,000,000 - $10,000,000 — 4.2%

OVER $10,000,000 — 6.6%

Source

to fight in Tax Court over a tax bill of $15,000 - $30,000. To the IRS, though, such a small sum is not worth the trouble and resources.

Several considerations go into how much of a fight you want to give over an audit, including the amount of money at stake and how solid your position is.

Audits are concluded in three ways:

1.) No change, meaning an audit in which you have substantiated all the items being reviewed and results in no changes.

2.) Agreed, meaning an audit the IRS proposed changes, and you understand and agree with the changes.

3.) Disagreed, meaning an audit the IRS proposed changes and you understand but disagree with the changes.

One of the most valuable assets we add for our clients is called an Audit Defense Plan. We meet with our clients at least twice a year: once at the end of the year to plan for the coming year and once in the spring, at tax time. We meet more if we need to, but we expect our clients to meet with us at least twice a year. We review the client's return for anything that stands out.

Walt: Having professionals on your side should be a key part of your strategy, both for developing your strategy and defending it.

There is another fundamental reason to have professionals involved. A new client of ours told me he went all the way through the audit level to the appeals level. He eventually settled. Nevertheless, by the time he factored in the entire spectrum of legal costs he incurred, he would have been better off settling the case on the front end. An experienced professional can advise you on whether your strategy will cost you more than it will save you.

To sum up, if you have properly reported your income and have a code-based reason and documentation for all your deductions, you have nothing to fear from an audit. But if you want to reduce your chances of an audit, you should have a strategy for legally reducing your adjusted gross income. It would be best if you did everything you can to reduce errors and inconsistencies in your returns. Furthermore, we advise you to avoid Schedule C income if possible. Avoid schemes the IRS has stated objections to, and consult with professionals, who can review your strategy for problems and deal with the IRS if an audit comes up.

Remember, the most effective defense to an audit is documentation and substantiation. Our audit review provides two important things for our clients:

1) We lower your risk of being audited.

2) If your number is pulled, we are well-organized and prepared to represent you in the process successfully.

In the next chapter, we will go over ways to organize a record-keeping system that will help ensure your documents are well-organized and ready for your CPA or the IRS to review.

④ KEY TAKEAWAYS

- IRS auditors are normal people focused on doing their jobs just like you and me. They typically don't have a personal axe to grind and will treat you with courtesy if you do the same for them.

- Your best friend in an audit is documentation and substantiation. The IRS can always disprove what you cannot prove, but they cannot disprove what you can prove.

- The greater your adjusted gross income, the greater your chances of an audit. Logically, the IRS wants to focus its limited resources where the greatest amount of money is concentrated.

▶ VIDEO RESOURCES

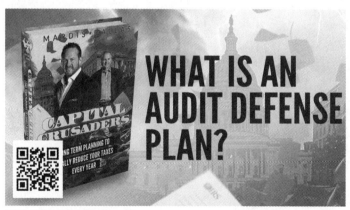

LINK: bit.ly/Crusaders34

JOHN MARSHALL

"THE POWER TO TAX
IS THE POWER TO
DESTROY."

DOCUMENTATION & COMPLIANCE

Walt: Proper documentation is the first step in defending yourself and successfully presenting your case to prevent it from moving to the appellate level. It is imperative to have your documents in order, period. From experience, most of our clients are engulfed in their work, documentation is often on the back burner, and they are merely guessing in their tax planning. They may not know which records to keep, nor are they assisted in creating a proper recording system. Good recordkeeping and the documentation of expenses is critical. Your records cannot be a mess when you turn them over to the IRS. They must be organized according to the receipts' dates, and you must be ready to act if an audit takes place.

Todd: One of the biggest fears surrounding an audit is being caught unprepared and flatfooted. You might think, "Holy smokes, I have to stop everything I'm doing and get organized!" This is a massive problem and can cause great stress to a business owner. On the other hand, the business owner who has everything properly organized is ready to deal with the audit.

Walt: Therefore, we discourage our clients from using the "shoebox" system. When the IRS pops open the top of your shoebox and sees the big mess of receipts and how nothing is organized, the audit will not work out very well for you.

> ## "YOUR RECORDS CANNOT BE A MESS WHEN YOU TURN THEM OVER TO THE IRS."
>
> WALT DALLAS

Todd: Think about it. If you were an IRS auditor, do you think you would be more apt to dig deep with sophisticated business owners who are producing exceptionally organized records? Or would you dig deeper with someone who is really struggling to come up with their receipts and does not have anything labeled?

Walt: To stress how important this is, we ended relationships with clients because they failed to maintain proper recordkeeping. If our clients refuse to keep up their records or fail to show up for our bi-annual meetings, we fire them. As a firm, we decided it is not worth risking, even when we lose their business. We want to win every time we are audited. We have a meager chance of winning if the client has little to no recordkeeping in place.

Todd: This kind of planning can be very successful, but as we mentioned in Chapter Four, sometimes IRS auditors will deny deductions simply because they have never seen them before. You must be prepared to document and substantiate a deduction an IRS auditor may not have experience with. You cannot expect them to take your word for it. You must be able to *show* them.

Walt: We met with a well-respected accounting firm of about twenty successful CPAs. The consensus was they liked what we were doing, and they understood it. Their only hesitation was they did not think their clients would keep proper records.

> **"WE WANT TO WIN EVERY TIME WE'RE AUDITED, AND WE HAVE A VERY LOW CHANCE OF WINNING IF THE CLIENT HAS LITTLE TO NO RECORDKEEPING IN PLACE."**
>
> WALT DALLAS

They were tired of stepping out on a limb with clients who refused to keep records.

Todd asked them if they provided their clients a system to document and file their records. Everyone lowered their heads because their expectations of poor recordkeeping were well-founded. They had not developed any such systems for their clients. How could this firm expect clients to keep records on very complex items when they had not provided their clients a system?

Todd: Every business owner should be using a system so they can back up certain deductions. If they state they earn a certain passive and/or active income, it is vital to prove it. They should show documentation demonstrating they work in a side job, the number of hours they work in that business, and their job responsibilities.

For example, if you own a profitable farm, but you are also using it as turkey hunting land, it is crucial to open a separate company with a separate checking account. Furthermore, you will need a business plan to conclusively demonstrate how it makes sense to keep the farm as an active, profit-turning business. When you have business expenses, you should document exactly what was performed to make those expenses deductible and demonstrate the benefit to your trade or business from that expense.

This book is designed to help you reduce your taxes legitimately and help you win if the IRS ever audits you due to your strategy or lack of understanding. We are committed to providing you the tools to succeed. We encourage you to share this commitment with us. That means you must do your part - keep your records and document. Your financial success depends on it. You cannot just hope you will keep good records. You might throw your receipts in a shoebox thinking you will organize it later, and it never happens. It is important to utilize a system and have someone hold you accountable.

Walt: We solve this issue because we have well-structured systems for our clients to use. Several years ago, Todd created a Documentation Assistance Program, also referred to as DAP. As an organization, we work diligently to improve it every year. We are continuously making it better, easier to use, and less time-consuming. This is how it works:

1) The client receives a weekly email to input their own data. This should only take 5-10 minutes of their time. This will document items such as hours spent on the business, activities, and meetings held.

2) The client emails the information to our accounting firm. From there, the data is filed on the appropriate IRS-conforming substantiation forms.

3) At the end of the month, the client will receive a summary

of the data.

4) At the end of the year, the information is provided to the client's CPA, and returns are filed.

With the technology available to you and with the system you will develop, your receipts will store in the appropriate folder right away. Because you can take pictures with your phone and store permanent records in correctly-labeled electronic folders, you will always stay organized should that day with the IRS ever come.

There are certain ways to document a deduction so it will pass the IRS substantiation rules. For most deductions, substantiation will be similar: you should document the day, time, location, the people present, and the business purpose - which is perhaps the most important component. Enter it into a form that will be immediately accessible. It should also be of good quality. Many people keep physical receipts, and those receipts can fade over time, which is yet another pitfall of keeping receipts in a shoebox. If you cannot tell what a receipt says, the IRS sure can't.

> "WHEN EVERYTHING IS THOROUGHLY DOCUMENTED, WITH NO GRAY AREA, WHEN EVERY LAST DEDUCTION IS BACKED WITH SPECIFICS FROM THE TAX CODE, THE AUDITOR CAN'T ARGUE WITH YOU."
>
> TODD MARDIS

Todd: There are different tools and apps available to the public, but no one, as far as I know, has a program as extensive as ours. We dedicate an immense amount of time to the different services we provide your business, what expenses are legally deductible, and ways you can offset your income when employee benefits are deemed deductible. Our system proves to the IRS that our clients qualify for all the fringe benefits because

DOCUMENTATION OF DEDUCTIONS

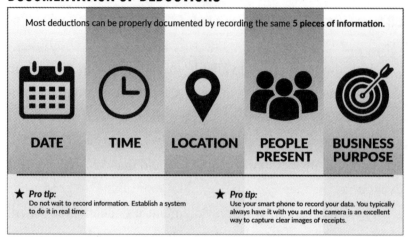

Most deductions can be properly documented by recording the same **5 pieces of information.**

DATE   **TIME**   **LOCATION**   **PEOPLE PRESENT**   **BUSINESS PURPOSE**

★ **Pro tip:**
Do not wait to record information. Establish a system to do it in real time.

★ **Pro tip:**
Use your smart phone to record your data. You typically always have it with you and the camera is an excellent way to capture clear images of receipts.

we run to the Tax Code and maintain proper documentation for substantiation.

When you are developing your recordkeeping system, think about what will demonstrate your best case in front of an IRS auditor. When everything is thoroughly documented, with no gray area, when every deduction is backed with specifics from the Tax Code, we have a much higher chance of winning an audit. That is why recordkeeping is so crucial.

Depending on the number of events the business owner has had each week - events where recordkeeping and documentation are necessary - proper documentation should take 5-10 minutes per week.

Walt: This is a small investment of one's time. Every businessperson can spare 5-10 minutes a week to protect their business income. Our goal is to position people to the point where they are at peace because they are prepared and organized. One of the most unpleasant things about the audit is digging up the old records. If you do not manage a good system, you will be digging for a long time.

Todd: As we create your plan, we will also explain which records to keep. If you maintain a plan for organizing and labeling them, that is even better! When it is tax time, you will deliver all of these records to your CPA. You will want everything to be clear, so they will know what you are attempting to accomplish.

A few CPAs may view what we do as pushing the envelope because they might not understand what we do. Yes, we are assertive when it comes to pushing a legitimate, code-based deduction. We found the IRS is much more likely to accept our strategies when producing records from our Document Assistance Program and the pair of annual meetings with the client. Many CPAs commonly accept a client's representation that business expenses are valid - when the client may or may not verify any of what he claims as deductions.

Walt: In that scenario, the CPA is the one pushing the envelope. Accepting expenses without proper documentation is a big risk. We do not work in this way because we do not want to risk losing a potential audit.

Once you have your recordkeeping plan in place, you will share those records with your CPA so they can file your tax returns. Your CPA is a valuable part of your tax planning team, but there are things your CPA probably cannot do for you. In the next chapter, we will review what your CPA might not be telling you - and why.

⑤ KEY TAKEAWAYS

The everyday systems within your business should naturally have you organized and ready in the event of an audit. Such systems prevent much of the anxiety associated with a potential audit because all the pieces for your successful defense are already in place.

Properly designed documentation procedures should not require more than a 5-10 minute investment each week by the business owner.

▶ VIDEO RESOURCES

LINK: bit.ly/Crusaders6

LINK: bit.ly/Crusaders23

HUGO BLACK

"THE UNITED STATES HAS A SYSTEM OF TAXATION BY CONFESSION."

WHAT YOUR CPA MAY NOT BE TELLING YOU, AND WHY

Todd: CPAs are an integral part of your professional team and offer support in achieving your financial goals. They possess a terrific skill set, and we rely on them in various forms with every client. However, they may not be able to fully assist you in a tax savings plan.

Walt: Your CPA has a great base of knowledge, and much effort goes into preparing and filing tax returns. As a group, CPAs are skilled professionals, and we give them a lot of credit for what they do. However, they should not be the only professional you work with to develop a robust financial tax plan. To achieve this, it is important to add a tax attorney to your team.

If you ask most CPAs how to save on taxes, they will typically advise you to fund a retirement plan or purchase a piece of heavy equipment and depreciate it. Those are the standard answers we receive, and each has its advantages and disadvantages. These strategies are implemented at the end of the year, and this form of planning is reactive. Our form of planning is proactive, as we understand your tax liability and plan ahead of the year to mitigate taxes.

Todd: From my experience, CPAs who are cautious by nature are unwilling to step out and act in a way they consider financially aggressive when advising their clients. We do not believe it is aggressive to follow the U.S. Tax Code to educate and assist our clients. We have worked with CPAs who tend to back away from a new concept or idea if they have not tried it, researched it, or even heard of it. They have liability when it comes to the tax returns of their clients. This encourages them to remain cautious and less willing to step out of their comfort zones.

> "IT ISN'T AGGRESSIVE TO FOLLOW THE U.S. TAX CODE IN EDUCATING AND ASSISTING OUR CLIENTS."
>
> TODD MARDIS

Walt: There is an economic reason CPAs might not step out of their comfort zone. The preparation of tax returns has become somewhat of a commodity, especially now since CPAs compete with computer software. Even with complex returns, many people who were never able to file tax returns can do so. People are not willing to pay as much to hire someone to file their tax returns. Now that a CPA might not charge as much and it is a flat rate, there is no benefit to spending the time to research tax-saving strategies.

Todd: One of the things we noticed in creating our own accounting firm is how time-consuming accounting is. In addition to the returns, the bookkeeping and payroll sides of client finances are overwhelming. I believe CPAs would love to provide you with tax strategies. Nonetheless, they quite frankly lack time to read case studies, know the rules, study new cases, and then apply the Tax Code to every client on an individual basis.

A CPA may retain one hundred or more clients. Capital Preservation Services works with the top 1-2% of income-earners in the country. Our planning process does not make sense for those who earn below a certain income threshold. Therefore, our target market is different from a typical CPA, who can work with anyone. Out of a CPA's hundred-plus clients, only a small handful will be in the top 1-2% of income-earners. We assist clients across the country, so we meet many CPAs. It is not unheard of to run into those who are progressive and think outside the box. Those CPAs tend to have more clients in the top 1-2% of income earners, and they partner with firms like ours. They know

> "OUT OF A CPA'S 250-400 CLIENTS, ONLY A SMALL HANDFUL IS GOING TO BE IN THE TOP 1-2 PERCENT OF INCOME-EARNERS."
>
> TODD MARDIS

the top income-earners will jump at the chance to discuss proven techniques that will deliver immediate and long-lasting tax savings.

An average CPA competing with software programs to earn average wage-earners' business must be efficient. How efficient would it be for the CPA to recreate their entire business model for the sake of, maybe, one or two of their one hundred clients?

Walt: Why would a CPA invest extra time and risk extra liability to learn and implement a strategy that will not give them any economic benefit? Therefore, specialized tax planning is generally outside the realm of what CPAs offer their clients. That kind of work can become a big drain on their time, as they are already under considerable pressure to meet deadlines. They certainly do not want to spend extra time on something when it will not generate any additional revenue.

Todd: There is an adage that we don't know what we don't know, meaning we do not even understand what knowledge we are missing. Because your CPA lacks time to learn all the different strategies and typically does not study specialized tax planning, they simply are not familiar with it and might shy away from these techniques. This does not mean the CPA does not want to save the client's money. They absolutely care if the client saves money on taxes - everyone wants to save on their tax burden. Unfortunately, this is not the kind of tax planning most CPAs are familiar with.

For instance, many of our strategies require us to restructure a client's business. The restructuring allows us to implement certain tax codes within a plan. Tax attorneys are needed for this process and understand what can be achieved.

> "IT'S MUCH BETTER TO REFUSE TO TRY A TECHNIQUE WITH OTHER PEOPLE'S FINANCES IF YOU DON'T UNDERSTAND IT THAN IT IS TO GIVE IT A GREEN LIGHT IF YOU DON'T KNOW HOW TO EXECUTE IT."
>
> WALT DALLAS

Walt: These are high-level legal concepts. Therefore, they require a tax attorney and legal team for implementation. Sometimes, when a CPA sees this plan for the first time, they are unsure of it simply because they may not know how to execute it, and their hands are legally tied. If they do not understand it, the easy way is to refuse to try a technique with other people's finances.

Todd: The best advice would be to go for it because of the tax savings involved and the representation you receive from our legal firm.

Walt: Another reason CPAs might be unsure of this form of planning is how they are trained. They are trained not to venture into seemingly aggressive areas. You are talking about having to establish arguments to justify and defend everything you do.

When you take a deduction or create a structure, you must build a defense. Think of it as a legal case you are constructing. We learned how to prove what we are doing fits the tests as defined by the law. Is there evidence, and is it reasonable? Once we answer those questions, we build the case through the documentation. It is a skill that all attorneys learn in law school.

> "CPAS ARE TRAINED TO BE CONSERVTIVE. THEY'RE TRAINED NOT TO VENTURE INTO AGGRESSIVE AREAS."
>
> WALT DALLAS

Additionally, I studied accounting. CPAs learn things such as how the financial segments are drawn together in accounting school, which is a challenge. On the other hand, you *do not* learn how to document major deductions. You do not really learn how to prove or create something that will stand up years down the road. By then, everyone has most likely forgotten about the transaction, and the only thing left is the documentation you created. While CPAs are trained to justify and defend their position, they are not trained like attorneys. Attorneys learn about proving cases and study the ever-changing tax laws and codes, which is the kind of training we are referring to.

For instance, Section 7701(o) was passed over a year ago. That provision says transactions must meet certain tests, such as the old "economics substance/business judgment" rule - for any

HOW AMERICANS FILE THEIR TAXES

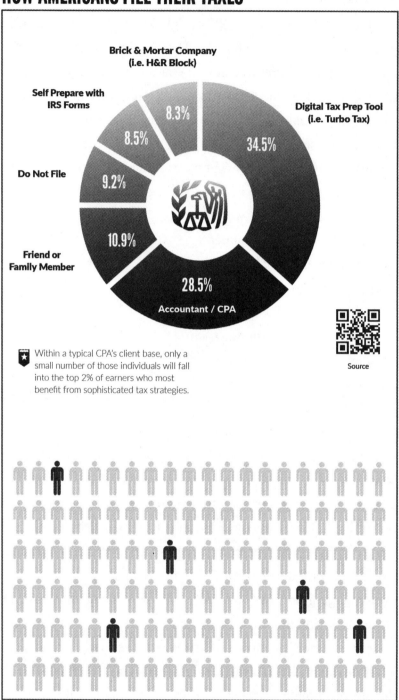

Brick & Mortar Company
(i.e. H&R Block)

Self Prepare with
IRS Forms

Digital Tax Prep Tool
(i.e. Turbo Tax)

8.3%

8.5%

34.5%

Do Not File

9.2%

10.9%

Friend or
Family Member

28.5%

Accountant / CPA

Within a typical CPA's client base, only a small number of those individuals will fall into the top 2% of earners who most benefit from sophisticated tax strategies.

Source

item you deduct, you must demonstrate a proper business purpose. This has been the rule for a long time, but Section 7701(o) added an additional requirement. The new rule states transactions must be different, before vs. after. This one is a bit more difficult to document because we must show how something has substantively changed from what it was in the first place. Plus, it must prove economic substance.

There is a related Section 162, which deals with deductions and the concept of "ordinary and necessary," according to the definition handed down by the U.S. Supreme Court. This code says the transaction must establish fair market value. If you make payments to an independent third party, you are in good shape, but if you engage in a related-party transaction, which happens many times in our planning, you must ensure the items are being charged at fair market value.

Items are built into our plans designed to prove if something is ordinary or fair market value. Sometimes we need a rental rate on a home that is rented for legitimate business purposes, and we need to ensure the rental is within the range of reasonable, fair market value. We hire independent appraisers to prove the rental rate is, in fact, fair market value, and it is a necessary expense. The U.S. Supreme Court has said necessary means it must be *helpful* to the business.

> "THE CPA ISN'T LICENSED TO PRACTICE LAW AND THEREFORE CAN'T IMPLEMENT CERTAIN STRATEGIES."
>
> WALT DALLAS

Todd: It may be easy to read the Tax Codes, but no one should ever try to rewrite them; you simply need the Tax Code as a backup in whatever you do. Ask yourself, does the transaction meet codes Sections 7701 and 162?

Walt: That can be challenging for our CPA friends who did not attend law school and may not be comfortable dealing with certain tax codes. The fact is our kind of tax planning requires a good bit of law practice mixed with good planning and carefully thought-out business structures. Your CPA, no matter how qualified, just does not possess this kind of expertise. They are not licensed to practice law and therefore cannot implement certain strategies. We highly encourage our clients to give their CPAs grace when they do not assist with tax deductions.

> "WE DON'T WANT TO MAKE YOUR CPA SEEM LIKE THEY AREN'T DOING THEIR JOB IF THEY AREN'T SAVING YOU MONEY. THAT'S THE WHOLE POINT—THAT'S NOT REALLY THEIR JOB."
>
> TODD MARDIS

Todd: A successful consultant summarized the difference between the CPA and a tax attorney this way: You present something to the CPA they are unaware of, and they say, "No." You present the same unknown thing to the tax attorney, and they say, "Let me see." Ultimately, they work to find a way.

When CPAs and tax attorneys are sitting on the same side of the table, you win. CPAs do not write legal documents or implement tax strategies, and tax attorneys like Walt do not file tax returns, so it's a relationship for the client that builds momentum and strength when combined.

Oftentimes, clients love our plan but request we run it by their CPA. Our answer may surprise people. We simply answer, "No." We do not review our plans with the client's CPAs. Honestly, we will not change the mind of a CPA who has been in business for several years in a meeting of 15-20 minutes. It takes hours and hours to go through the details about the innerworkings of a plan that has been tweaked and modified to ensure the Code has been satisfied. We learned this lesson the hard way. In the past, we became bogged down when working with an individual's CPA.

Walt: Of course, this does not mean your CPA is not allowed to participate in your tax planning process. Once you decide to become a client of ours, your CPA is invited to every meeting.

Quite often, CPAs confide they are frustrated with their own careers because they have been unable to offer many tax-saving strategies. Once they begin working with us, they are excited to be part of a team that can save their clients real money.

Todd: Continue to work with your CPA as we develop your strategy. They should be part of your team because you need tax returns completed accurately. It would be best to ensure they are prepared to incorporate our tax strategies into your returns.

Walt: As we mentioned several times, keeping your CPA on board is an integral part of your plan. This is because your CPA is the person who will report what you do to the IRS. In the next chapter, we will tell you something you should *not* do when developing your plan: tie your CPA's hands when it comes to your tax returns.

KEY TAKEAWAYS

The time-intensive tasks of properly and accurately reporting your financial activity at the end of the year often leave the CPA little to no time to evaluate the nuances of the Tax Code or to perform complex future planning for their high-net worth clients.

Many tax-planning techniques require the ability to argue facts as applied to the Tax Code. Such a skill set is more typically found in tax lawyers than with CPAs.

Many tax-planning techniques require the restructuring of a business. Once again, such knowledge and experience is more typically found in the legal world than the accounting world.

CPAs are required to process large amounts of data and transactions, often in a short period of time, when preparing a client's tax returns. To make such an effort profitable, the CPA's systems must be highly efficient, and typically do not adapt well to "coloring outside the lines."

Tax planning produces the best results with individuals in the top 1-2% of all income-earners. Due to the relatively small number of such individuals, most CPAs do not have the opportunity to study the unique needs and opportunities within that elite group.

▶VIDEO RESOURCES

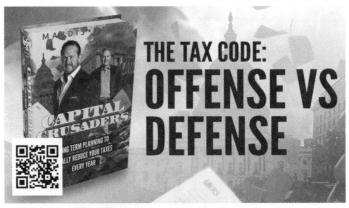

LINK: bit.ly/Crusaders7

LINK: bit.ly/Crusaders8

CALVIN COOLIDGE

"COLLECTING MORE TAXES
THAN IS ABSOLUTELY NECESSARY
IS LEGALIZED ROBBERY."

Your CPA's hands are legally tied
(Offense vs. Defense)

Todd: Taxpayers usually feel like they are on the defensive side of things when it comes to their taxes. They are unsure of what deductions the rules allow them to take, and others may not know what counts as income. Some look at their K-1 form and scratch their heads, while others do not even read their tax return. Therefore, people do not have a handle on where they are, much less where they are going. From that standpoint, of course, they are on defense.

Your situation is worse if you are audited. You must produce records you might not understand, and it is likely you have not approved the substantiation or grasped what it meant. When we engage new clients, it is typical to find they have maintained little to no recordkeeping in the past. The auditor inevitably asks for more documents, and people often struggle to come up with what the auditor is requesting. Now, they are *really* on defense.

Walt: Even when you know your CPA and tax attorney are good people who are working very hard for you, it is easy to worry about how much you will have to pay in taxes, *plus* how much this team of advisors might cost you. This is another example of being on defense: it is difficult to concentrate on exploring strategies to lessen your tax burden when you frequently think about the expenses you are running up with your CPA or tax attorney. The meter is running, and you are almost afraid to see the final bill.

Todd: To add to your frustration in audit situations, the auditor might propose something you will disagree with. You have a choice to challenge the ruling and move to the next level. However, this means more expense and no guarantee of a win. Suddenly it hits you right between the eyes and you say, "I know I'm on defense. I don't get to settle. I can't even punt the ball, and I'm too far out to try a field goal." No one can feel good in that situation.

Walt: Part of this scenario involves your CPA recording the tax deductions you set up in your returns. We mentioned this in previous chapters, but most of the time, people reach the end of the tax year and *then* start looking for deductions. At that point, the hay is already in the barn. It is too late

> "PEOPLE REACH THE END OF THE TAX YEAR AND THEN START LOOKING FOR DEDUCTIONS. AT THAT POINT, THE HAY IS ALREADY IN THE BARN."
>
> WALT DALLAS

to do anything new or different and too late to go on offense. All the CPA can do is accurately report what has already happened in the previous twelve months because neither you nor the CPA thought about this day *eighteen* months ago.

Todd: CPAs begin asking for financial documents, business expenses, and receipts in February and March. If this is when you start looking for ways to save on your taxes, there is absolutely no way to play offense. Playing defensively can frustrate many people. Sometimes, they will make bad decisions at the end of the year - such as ill-fated attempts to reduce their tax liabilities by spending a dollar to save forty cents. They say you can win football games with defense, but you simply cannot save taxes if you are continually in a defensive position.

Walt: Therefore, we train our clients to remain on the offensive. We teach them the rules in advance and give them an operational structure. Todd's documentation system is user-friendly and has consistently proven to meet the IRS substantiation tests. The IRS will not fight to the death on every little thing. They want to know individuals are playing by the U.S. Tax Code rules and showing thorough documentation for their transactions. If you know the rules and keep good records, you can be on offense.

> "WE TRAIN OUR CLIENTS TO GO ON THE OFFENSIVE. WE TEACH THEM THE RULES IN ADVANCE AND GIVE THEM AN OPERATIONAL STRUCTURE."
>
> WALT DALLAS

First, know what you can and cannot deduct. Once you have a good strategy and sound corporate structures, you will be deducting things you never imagined possible. You will grin from ear to ear because you will save real money in strict compliance with the Tax Code. That really makes you feel like you are on offense - and will be for the foreseeable future. This will give you a great deal of confidence as you make decisions.

Even better, once you engage professionals who understand how the Tax Code works - both your CPA and your tax attorneys - you will have a team of knowledgeable professionals on your side of the table year-round, including during an audit. The tax attorney will explain the strategies to the IRS auditor, point out the applicable tax codes, and provide every last keystroke of substantiation associated with the audit. I promise, as you watch it unfold, you will breathe a lot easier.

Walt: Our clients move through the year meeting with our attorneys and CPAs on ways to reduce their taxes, and they accomplish this before December 31. We have a very strategic meeting at year's end where we project their liabilities, incomes, and future expenses. We then begin implementing offensive strategies to reduce those liabilities legally. We cannot stress the idea of advanced planning enough. If you fail to plan well in advance, you are figuratively tying your CPA's hands.

> "IF YOU DON'T PLAN WELL IN ADVANCE, YOU ARE LITERALLY TYING YOUR CPA'S HANDS."
>
> WALT DALLAS

Todd: We see many individuals who seem to stay in a defensive mode all the time, and when we ask what their plan is, they say, "I have a CPA." Still, the clients who are meeting with us during the year to discuss reducing their taxes, the ones who are researching and thinking about it are the ones who are on offense. Think of it as being active vs. being passive. When there is a lot of money on the line, active is a much better approach.

Walt: It is never a good feeling to receive a call from a CPA who reveals you owe another $40,000 in taxes. People who do the kind of tax planning we are talking about do not receive

THE CPA VS THE TAX ATTORNEY AND WHY YOU NEED BOTH

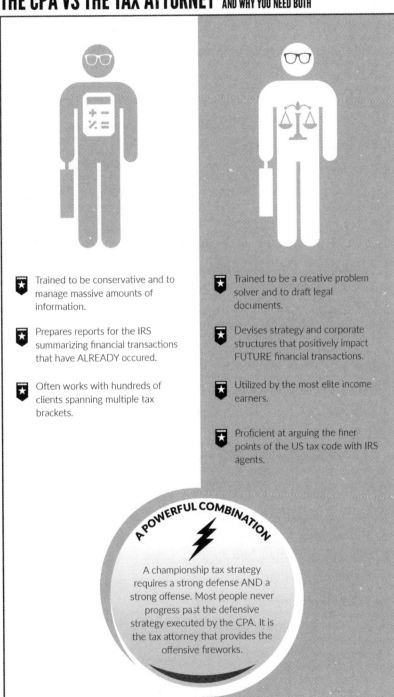

Trained to be conservative and to manage massive amounts of information.

Prepares reports for the IRS summarizing financial transactions that have ALREADY occured.

Often works with hundreds of clients spanning multiple tax brackets.

Trained to be a creative problem solver and to draft legal documents.

Devises strategy and corporate structures that positively impact FUTURE financial transactions.

Utilized by the most elite income earners.

Proficient at arguing the finer points of the US tax code with IRS agents.

A POWERFUL COMBINATION

A championship tax strategy requires a strong defense AND a strong offense. Most people never progress past the defensive strategy executed by the CPA. It is the tax attorney that provides the offensive fireworks.

such calls. After exploring many ways to reduce the client's taxes as low as possible, we have successfully predicted the tax liability. Yes, you will spend a little more time with your tax burden through the year than you used to, but it will save you a lot of money.

Todd: There's more to it than just proactively planning. You can do all the advanced planning in the world, but your CPA is still limited if you do not do it well.

For example, let's say an individual earns $500,000 in gross taxable income, and she needs $200,000 to run her house smoothly to pay household bills, set money aside for retirement, and pay her children's college tuition. She has performed well as she planned for $200,000 in tax write-offs. Yet that means over half of her income is taxable, and all her CPA can do is report income and calculate the bill. On the other hand, a person who develops a strategy to drop the income by planning and consulting with a tax attorney will be better off. The individual can restructure the remaining $300,000 to reduce the tax burden on the additional income, or even postpone the tax on it until it is at a lower rate while keeping plenty of money to maintain her monthly living expenses. Now *that* is going on the offensive.

Walt: As we mentioned before, we have a planning meeting with our clients to review the next year's plan. Keep in mind your plan needs to account for the fact that your situation can change. You might have children. They will grow up and move on to college. If you incorporate those life changes into your plan, you can work those kinds of

> "YOU CAN MITIGATE YOUR TAX BURDEN BY USING THE LAWS AS THEY ARE WRITTEN. THAT'S WHAT THEY'RE FOR."
>
> WALT DALLAS

LEGAL VS ILLEGAL THE SAFETY OF THE TAX CODE

Think of the US tax code as a castle. Remaining within the confines of the castle keeps you safe.

Tax strategy based in the code is ALWAYS legal.

TAX CODE

Tax strategy based in the code can still involve risk. But risk is based on individual circumstances, not legalities.

Venturing outside the tax code becomes both illegal and, obviously, greatly increases risk factors. Such actions should NEVER be part of your tax strategy.

ILLEGAL   **GREATER RISK**

deductions into your future. Your plan is not going to be static. It should change with your needs, which is another reason you need to stay ahead of your tax returns.

People have questioned our form of planning and labeled it too aggressive. Our question for them is, "How can it be aggressive to use what's in the U.S. Tax Code?" You can mitigate your tax burden by using the laws as they are written.

Todd: I would not call it aggressive. We are working with business practices and, of course, adhering strictly to what is provably and demonstrably written in the U.S. Tax Code. Hence, it is 100% legal, every single time.

Walt: This does not mean there is no risk. This kind of

planning does have some risk, but it is not the kind of risk that will keep you up at night. In the crucial year-end meeting, where the rubber really meets the road, we are doing a lot of work with our CPAs and fine-tuning the numbers to ensure we know the exact effect of the deduction to receive maximum benefit. The client definitely recognizes the feeling of being on offense, but it's not a situation where the client still feels like they're on the verge of falling off a cliff. There are risks involved, but we explain them, and the client always has the option to decline to take the risk. When this happens, we never argue - we immediately look for other strategies that may have inherent risks but will be more palatable to the client's risk capacity. The risk is the deduction may be disallowed, not that any nefarious or criminal activity occurred.

Todd: To be clear, the risk Walt is referring to is not at all whether the deductions are legal in the eyes of the federal government. With the proper substantiation, we are on solid footing. Some of these tax deductions result in fairly large benefits, so we

> "AS LONG AS THE DEDUCTION IS IN THE TAX CODE AND YOU'RE FOLLOWING THE LETTER OF THE LAW, YOU'LL WIN."
>
> TODD MARDIS

may have to argue the point. So long as the deduction is in the Tax Code and we follow the law, the odds of winning an audit drastically increase.

Our kind of planning takes a lot of work. But if you are paying too much in taxes, it is worth the effort.

Walt: We mentioned that some tax strategies have risk. Since risk seems to be a point of initial concern with most people we deal with, we will discuss techniques you might implement to mitigate such risks in the next chapter.

The Tax Code provides ways to reduce tax liabilities, but nothing is without risk.

Risk, like taxes, can be reduced with proper documentation.

KEY TAKEAWAYS

Planning is critical for offensive success.

The Tax Code provides ways to reduce tax liabilities, but nothing is without risk.

Risk, like taxes, can be reduced with proper documentation.

▶ VIDEO RESOURCES

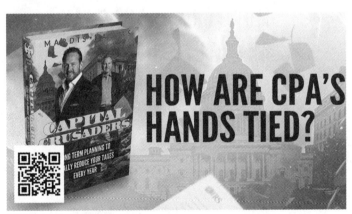

LINK: bit.ly/Crusaders9

BARRY GOLDWATER

"THE INCOME TAX CREATED
MORE CRIMINALS THAN
ANY OTHER SINGLE ACT
OF GOVERNMENT."

TAX MITIGATION STRATEGIES TO HANDLE WITH CARE

Todd: You should never place all your eggs in one basket. If you count on only one strategy to solve your tax mitigation problems, that raises a red flag. You generally want to use more strategies and tackle the issue in a variety of ways. One significant deduction on your tax return catches the attention of the IRS and could trigger an audit. We like to use multiple strategies, then ensure they all fit together in an excellent clean package, leaving nothing to stick out like a sore thumb.

Most people enter transactions knowing there are tax benefits behind those transactions, not understanding what Walt and I discussed earlier in the book, namely the transaction's economic substance and reasonableness. This is where most people fall into a trap.

People may blame advisors for bad advice. Sure, some advisors unintentionally make harmful recommendations, but most advisors don't intentionally lead people down the wrong path. Sometimes, we see people taking strategies and expanding them beyond their original intent. It is essential to understand the strategy, the pitfalls of pushing a con-

> "PEOPLE GET INTO TROUBLE WHEN THEY TRY TO PUSH A CONCEPT TOO FAR BEYOND ITS ORIGINAL INTENT."
>
> WALT DALLAS

cept too far, the advantages, how to utilize it properly, and how you can protect yourself.

A 412(i) plan is a defined-benefit pension plan designed for small business owners. It is a tax-qualified benefit plan, so any amount the owner contributes to the plan becomes available immediately as a tax deduction to the company. The owner can fund the plan with guaranteed annuities or a combination of annuities and life insurance.

Although this plan provides excellent retirement benefits, business owners were stretching beyond the rules and depositing large contributions, then rolling them out during periods in which there were no surrender penalties. They might have a million dollars in the account, but only $200,000 was not under surrender penalties. They would then withdraw $200,000 after a year or two, pay the tax on it, and not be required to pay any taxes on the remaining $800,000. As you can imagine, this is deeply frowned upon by the IRS.

Walt: The Tax Code's 419 Welfare Benefit Trusts was initially intended to be a death benefit plan funded by cash-value life insurance policies. You can own life insurance inside 419

BEWARE OF PUSHING BEYOND ORIGINAL INTENT

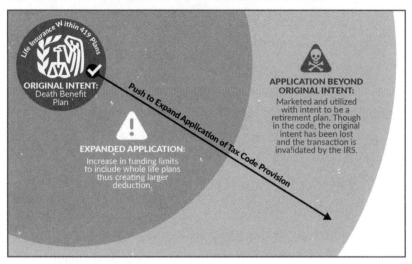

plans, but they must be death benefits.

People pushed to increase the funding of 419 plans to a substantial amount to accommodate whole life policies, creating large deductions. The problem was it turned what was intended to be a death benefit plan, which is allowable under the Code, into a retirement plan. Of course, the promoters were very careful not to call it a retirement plan, but when the marketers heard of it, suddenly people called it what it was - a retirement plan. Predictably, the term began showing up in the marketing brochures, and when people began funding these plans, they intended to do exactly what the brochure said: fund a retirement plan. Intent is a significant factor. Everyone lost the concept in the Code, which was this plan could only be a death benefit. I represented several people who purchased these and needed help unwinding them.

Todd: The conservation easement is a noble idea and allows for significant deductions. An individual or group sets aside land and restricts the use of the land by creating green space. One of the positives is we are keeping property pristine. This strategy seems to play on both sides of the aisle: Republicans typically like it because the green space appeals to their constituents, such as land to hunt on, and it represents a smaller government because of the tax deductions. The Democrats tend to like it because of the green space, the conservations, and the anti-global warming aspect.

The tax deduction in conservation easements is based on an appraisal determining the loss of the property's highest and best use. You restrict the highest and best use in perpetuity, meaning the restriction can never leave the property for generations to come. The total acreage in private conservation easements is equal to approximately 80% of the total acreage set aside by the federal government in federal lands and parks.

There are two different types of conservation easements: a syndicated easement and a non-syndicated easement. The non-syndicated easement means you have owned a piece of property outright for at least a year and a day, and you decide to restrict the property.

The second form of a conservation easement would be a syndicated conservation easement. In this case, a group of investors purchases a piece of property they identified as possessing the highest and best use that could be restricted. Then they essentially create a real estate partnership and sell memberships. In those cases, the losses flow down to the members in proportion to their ownership.

Syndicated conservation easements have drawn more attention from the IRS, which is why you want to be extra careful with them. If you participate in a conservation easement, you must disclose on your tax return you participated because it is a listed transaction. As we discussed earlier in the book, just because something is a listed transaction does not mean it is illegal or wrong - it just means it has exceptional tax benefits, so the IRS will want to know about your participation.

When the IRS looks carefully at conservation easements, it is good for everyone. It cleans up the bad actors taking shortcuts and buying properties that did not retain the highest and best use of any kind. The second benefit of the IRS carefully monitoring them is the individuals who *do* play by the rules do so with the utmost care.

Walt: Conservation easements have excellent tax benefits, but it is imperative to maintain an independent business purpose beyond that. You want the property to retain a use, like fish or rice farming, to generate income. We reviewed many syndicated conservation easements that did not have any business purpose and were created merely for the sole purpose of taking a tax deduction. The project was halted, as there did not seem to be any other uses for the property.

Todd: Like anything with tax benefits, many individuals push the envelope. For example, John Smith has inherited fifty acres 300 miles from Dallas, Texas. This property is suitable for hunting and farming but not much else. However, he deploys a phony appraisal that declares the highest and best use would be high-end retail spaces with living areas on the second floor valued at ten million dollars. No one would ever develop a property in such a way when it is so far from a city of any size, so it is highly improbable the property is worth that much. If he places it into a conservation easement and attempts to take a deduction on the difference in value, it would be invalid.

This is where the problems come in with the highest and best use concerning conservation easements. People use misguided economic values, and then the IRS sends people to evaluate the price on the property to determine a real fair market value. They find it is not worth nearly as much as the report says it is.

Walt: Conservation easements involve a complex, very sophisticated strategy that can work extraordinarily well, but it must be completed by someone who knows how to accomplish it. Congress added Section 170(h) into the Tax Code to encourage conservation and encourage people to conserve properties. That said, the people making the conservation (especially in the syndicated arena) must be diligent and organized - if anything is inaccurate, it can nullify the deduction.

There must be a qualified real property interest, which is a legally defined term. You should also be able to explain the interest being transferred. The property needs to be deeded to a qualified organization, and it must be completed exclusively for conversation purposes. The wording in the deed must be exact, and the protection must be in perpetuity.

We spotted a case recently where the deed was *not* in perpetuity, and an enormous deduction was denied - all because a couple of words were not quite right in the deed. Just a couple of words, and suddenly this entire complicated, sophisticated structure designed to save the investor a lot of money fell short when the IRS challenged him.

Todd: Let's say I own fifty acres in the middle of Telluride, Colorado. A developer approaches me with an offer to develop this land by building condominiums and high-end retail shops on the bottom floor. I could earn twenty million dollars from this property in the next ten years after being developed. I decide I do not want to destroy the habitat in the area. There are elk, red fox, and other wildlife in the area, and I really like the green space. I don't want concrete, nor do I want to create a carbon footprint on my fifty acres, so I decide to participate in

CONSERVATION EASEMENTS RESTRICTING THE HIGHEST AND BEST USE OF LAND

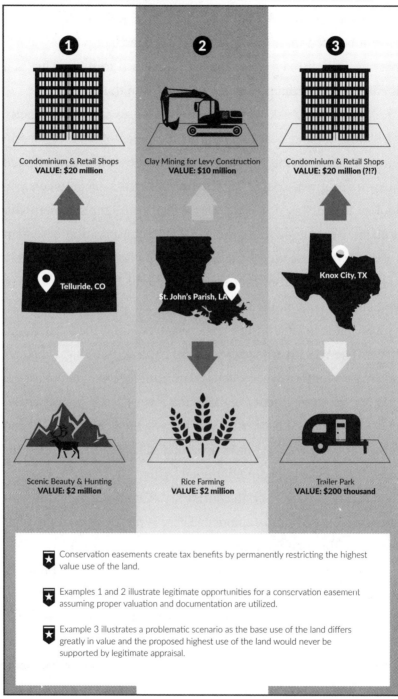

1

Condominium & Retail Shops
VALUE: $20 million

Telluride, CO

Scenic Beauty & Hunting
VALUE: $2 million

2

Clay Mining for Levy Construction
VALUE: $10 million

St. John's Parish, LA

Rice Farming
VALUE: $2 million

3

Condominium & Retail Shops
VALUE: $20 million (?!?)

Knox City, TX

Trailer Park
VALUE: $200 thousand

Conservation easements create tax benefits by permanently restricting the highest value use of the land.

Examples 1 and 2 illustrate legitimate opportunities for a conservation easement assuming proper valuation and documentation are utilized.

Example 3 illustrates a problematic scenario as the base use of the land differs greatly in value and the proposed highest use of the land would never be supported by legitimate appraisal.

an easement. The easement declares my fifty acres can never be commercially or residentially developed in perpetuity. That significantly devalues the property because now it is just dirt. It cannot be used for anything else. My property previously worth twenty million may now only be worth *two* million. This is a legitimate tax deduction of eighteen million dollars.

Many people ask why you would want to strip the property of its highest and best use. You own a piece of high net-worth property, permanently remove its value for a tax write-off, and keep it for green space. This might not make sense when you look at it that way. Consider this scenario we encountered with a client: Years ago, we participated in a conservation easement for a client where we restricted mining a particular type of clay called "borrow" from a property in central Louisiana. To give you a little context, the Corps of Engineers partnered with individual states to rebuild the levee systems along the Mississippi River. The river is often affected by chronic flooding, which is one reason for the levee systems' deterioration. As it happens, the number one component to rebuild the levee system is the borrow clay. We identified properties and farms which could be sold and mined as borrow pits. I have seen pictures of farms stripped for clay, and they are absolutely ruined. After it is mined from more than eighty feet beneath the surface, it becomes a giant mud pit and looks like a bomb exploded. There is no living creature over the entire three hundred acres.

On the other hand, there were other things these property owners *could* do. One of the properties was being used as a rice farm. There were also hunting leases associated with the farm. When the rice was harvested, they flooded the land and used it to farm crawfish. Other uses for the property still made it valuable, but the highest and best use was to strip the property and remove the clay.

Therefore, retaining other uses is what potentially makes conservation easements a good move for property owners. They can utilize a tax write-off by removing a use that might not appeal to them and still retain other property uses.

Walt: There are even more regulatory requirements when there is a mining operation on a property in a conservation easement. You must adhere to the surface mining provisions, retain mortgage subordination, baseline documentation, and your reports must be very carefully constructed. The appraisal is critical - this determines the property's value and deduction amount.

In those cases, you calculate the value of a mine on a property, then add a restriction. This could be any restriction, but the most common restriction is *not* to mine the property. As a result, you are taking away one of the most powerful economic tools of the property - you are removing the ability to mine. The valuation goes from an exceptionally high number to a very modest number, and the difference in valuation is going to be the amount of the deduction. Again, the appraisal is critical, especially in syndicated deals. Request multiple appraisals so you will not be relying on just one. We typically secure three appraisals to ensure those deductions were well-supported.

Another thing to consider when using these conservation easements would be protection.

Those who deal with conservation easements are much more careful than before. The appraisers are just as cautious because they know full well their work could be reviewed, and they know the appraisals need to be within 10-20% of the federal government's appraisal of the property. All of this has resulted in better, more accurate appraisals. If someone correctly completes everything from a technical standpoint and provides what the IRS considers a solid appraisal, the government will have a tough time denying the deduction. Sure, they could discount it, but it is a lot less likely when you acquire three appraisals.

A lot can go wrong in conservation easements because they are so precise, so it's always a good idea to protect yourself. What happens if your deduction is denied? To mitigate risk, insurance can be purchased to protect yourself and the conservation easements.

Todd: The insurance company willing to accept the risks of insuring our client's conservation easements is one of the world's largest and oldest. This company has been evaluating risks longer than the U.S.A. has been a country. This gives you an idea of the legitimacy of these kinds of deals.

Another strategy that needs to be handled with care is the private insurance company. It is a great strategy, but it does come with caveats. Private insurance companies are a way for business owners to mitigate risks internally. Section 501(c)(15) of the Tax Code says if a business owner has a risk they foresee as being able to damage their ability to stay in business or be profitable, the IRS will allow them to insure those risks. If you want to take advantage of the provision, set up a company to insure your risks.

This creates a nice tax deduction. Like other kinds of large deductions, though, people become aggressive with these. The IRS came down on a group in Atlanta, Georgia, for insuring against a bogus risk. Surgeons in the Atlanta area were insuring themselves against being kidnapped and held for ransom. Some professions run that risk, such as petroleum engineers in Africa. Still, the odds of a doctor in Buckhead being kidnapped and held for ransom are almost none. The IRS challenged them and won.

Suppose you choose an 831(b) election. In that case, it is

only available to corporations that qualify as non-life insurance companies. They must have a net or direct written premium, whichever is greater, that does not exceed the annual premium threshold level of $2.3 million and pass at least one of the two diversification tests. Once the election is made, the electing company must continue to meet the qualification criteria annually to continue to receive the election's benefits. Ultimately, before the IRS cracked down, we knew of those who set up insurance companies to move money out of businesses on a tax-deductible basis without adding any coverage in place that had any substantial risk.

Walt: Just like conservation easements, it requires a real business purpose to participate. If you form a captive just for tax purposes and there is no underlying business purpose, the transaction can be attacked. You must carefully review the whole transaction and lay the proper foundation. If you want to take advantage of this deduction, you must have a genuine business purpose and a real need for insurance to cover a real risk. You should *not* participate merely for income tax purposes.

In addition to those types of risks, one of the less obvious dangers of using captive insurance companies is that the term "insurance" is not defined in the Code. Furthermore, it is not outlined in the cases very well. This leaves a lot open to interpretation, which is inherently dangerous.

These strategies are suitable, but you must properly develop them and have an independent business purpose to back them up.

When you own a private insurance company, you pay insurance premiums to the company, and Section 162 allows you to take a deduction for those premiums. If you do not file a claim, you retain the premiums. That is a neat concept from a tax perspective; you take the tax deduction, *and* you keep the premiums, if you manage your risk. Later, when you sell your business, you shut down the insurance business, and you can access those dollars on a very efficient basis.

If this is a strategy you are considering, ask yourself a couple of questions: What is your business purpose? Why are you doing it? Preserve independent documentation that demonstrates you require a particular kind of insurance you cannot purchase anywhere else.

Several of our clients have been extremely interested in captive insurance companies just from an insurance standpoint. The tax benefits throw icing on the cake - they indeed end up with coverage through the captives they cannot participate in anywhere else. In a previous chapter, we mentioned the attorney who kept two million dollars in his trust account and could not find insurance to guard against employee theft. That risk may have been unlikely, but it was legitimate. He could purchase the insurance he needed through a captive, and the bonus was he received tax benefits.

Todd: Like conservation easements, if you use this strategy, you must satisfy clear-cut requirements. First, do *not* set it up where your pricing is determined in-house. Your pricing must be established outside of your organization, and it needs to be equivalent to premiums you would pay elsewhere.

Second, there must be separation. Many people who were cleaned out of business were setting up their own shops, issuing and pricing the coverages themselves and *reinsuring* the coverages themselves. The IRS disallowed all of them. Without any separation, there was no real risk mitigation, so it did not meet the test.

There must be actual risk shifting. Real risk shifting comes

CAPTIVE INSURANCE COMPANY A SOPHISTICATED AND POWERFUL TECHNIQUE

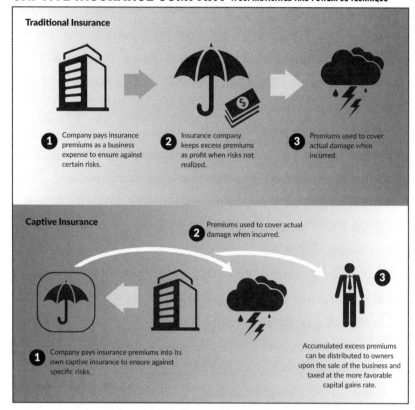

Traditional Insurance

1. Company pays insurance premiums as a business expense to ensure against certain risks.

2. Insurance company keeps excess premiums as profit when risks not realized.

3. Premiums used to cover actual damage when incurred.

Captive Insurance

2. Premiums used to cover actual damage when incurred.

1. Company pays insurance premiums into its own captive insurance to ensure against specific risks.

3. Accumulated excess premiums can be distributed to owners upon the sale of the business and taxed at the more favorable capital gains rate.

where you set up a reinsurance company. You are not just insuring your risks; you are insuring other individuals' risks, and you are all sharing the risk.

To illustrate, when you own an insurance policy and a claim has not been filed by the end of twelve months, you are happy because your insurance company has not increased your rates. They are pleased because they did not pay any claims. However, they do not refund your premiums. They keep them.

An example of how these captive insurance companies can be used: A pool of individuals who share common risks, such as physicians or a group of attorneys, pay for malpractice insurance or errors and omissions coverage. They never issue a claim on their respective insurance policies. They want to reduce their insurance premiums, so they collaborate and form their own captive - a risk pool. They keep their third-party insurance, but they set aside money in their captive. If one of them has a claim, the captive will pay the first $100,000 on the person's behalf. Then each person in the pool can raise their deductible on their third-party insurance to $100,000.

If you have a $100,000 deductible, everyone's premium decreases. Then, after 5-10 years of setting money aside to cover their risks, this same group of people with the same risk now has a surplus. Based on surplus, the group decides to raise the coverage to the first $250,000, further reducing the third-party premium. You can see how the risk pool would continue to grow, and at some point, they would not rely on third-party coverage at all.

Walt: This is the safe harbor that must be met: Is the risk real? Is the pricing accurate? Is the risk shared?

Todd: If you want to utilize either of these strategies, you need a tax attorney to help execute them. The requirements are precise, and the benefits are large enough that the IRS looks very closely at them. You need someone who knows how to construct these strategies to stand up to IRS scrutiny and defend you, should you ever be audited.

> "YOU SHOULD DEFINITELY TAKE SPECIAL CARE WITH COMPLICATED TRANSACTIONS THAT THE IRS MAY NOT BE FAMILIAR WITH."
>
> TODD MARDIS

Walt: As an indication of how much the IRS does not like private insurance companies, research their website. You will notice Section 501(c)(15) is labeled as "overcapitalization," and then it uses the term "stuffing transactions." They are really not too keen on these. There seems to be a special task force in the

IRS looking at private insurance companies. In the audits, many auditors are denying or discounting the deductions. These strategies have a very high chance of being audited and even denied for, sometimes, invalid reasons.

Todd: You should take care of these and other complicated transactions the IRS may not be familiar with. There is a good chance you will be audited, and a good chance the IRS will deny it just because they do not like it. However, if you engaged a tax attorney to structure it properly and manage your documentation and substantiation, you have a much higher chance of winning an appeal. Judges have scolded the IRS on multiple occasions for not following the Tax Code. Judges told them if they do not like the Tax Code, they can contact Congress and ask them to rewrite the laws. The IRS does not pass legislation - Congress does. The IRS may not like legislation because it has tax benefits, but that does not make the transaction any less legitimate.

Walt: We've spent a fair bit of time talking about less common tax savings strategies. No book about tax savings would be complete without talking about the more common methods for saving on your taxes. In the next chapter, we will discuss retirement plans and how different strategies are available for different needs.

⑧ KEY TAKEAWAYS

🗝 Multiple and varied strategies, rather than a single strategy, should be employed to achieve the highest level of tax savings.

🗝 The most common missteps often involve taking a valid strategy and then trying to expand it beyond its intended reach and purpose.

🗝 Some tax saving strategies (i.e. conservation easements, private insurance companies) are perfectly legal, but also highly sophisticated to execute. Trying to do so without the proper knowledge and experience can lead to disaster.

🗝 There are tax saving strategies the IRS clearly does not like and are thus more susceptible to being audited. However, just because the IRS does not like such transactions does not mean they aren't legal. Properly-structured strategies will always stand up to scrutiny.

▶ VIDEO RESOURCES

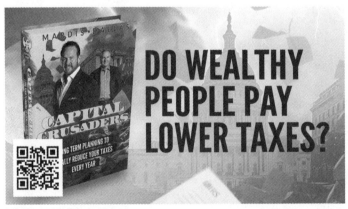

LINK: bit.ly/Crusaders10

LINK: bit.ly/Crusaders24

BENJAMIN FRANKLIN

"IN THIS WORLD
NOTHING IS CERTAIN BUT DEATH
AND TAXES."

UNDERSTANDING RETIREMENT STRATEGIES

Todd: When planning for retirement, there are multiple ways to fund your plan. An individual may rely on rental income, the sale of a business, looking to the tax benefits from life insurance, and distributions from a 401(k).

Walt: There are other suitable options, such as non-qualified deferred comp plans or brokerage accounts.

Todd: The term "retirement" refers to when you are no longer actively engaged in a day-to-day occupation. You are not drawing any W-2 or 1099 wages from active income. We are looking at forms of *passive* income.

An example of passive income is rental income, such as having homes or retaining rental income from a business you sell.

401K BEST AND WORST CASE SCENARIOS

Best Case

In this scenario the 28% tax bracket rate is avoided by placing money in the 401k during the "Present Day." When the 401k funds are withdrawn upon retirment they are taxed at the 25% tax bracket rate as: A) total income has decreased and B) taxes have remained constant.

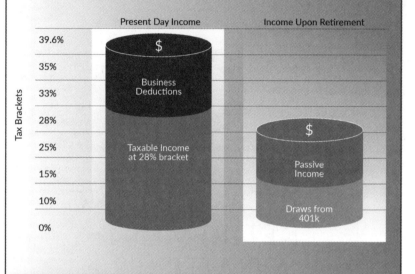

Present Day Income   Income Upon Retirement

Tax Brackets

| 39.6% |
| 35% |
| 33% |
| 28% |
| 25% |
| 15% |
| 10% |
| 0% |

$ Business Deductions

Taxable Income at 28% bracket

$ Passive Income

Draws from 401k

Worst Case

In this scenario a HIGHER rate of taxes (33% vs 28%) are being paid on draws from the 401k in retirement than what would have been paid on the same money as regular income during "Present Day." The discrepancy is due to: A) larger amount of passive income potentially casued by a lack of planning, and B) a rise in the tax rate. In such circumstances, the 401k was a bad investment!

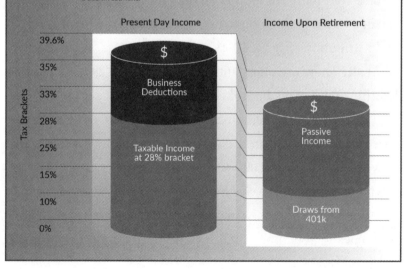

Present Day Income   Income Upon Retirement

Tax Brackets

| 39.6% |
| 35% |
| 33% |
| 28% |
| 25% |
| 15% |
| 10% |
| 0% |

$ Business Deductions

Taxable Income at 28% bracket

$ Passive Income

Draws from 401k

Another example is revenue from your business, either through a one-time sale or an installment plan. Then there are distributions from a 401(k) that many people rely upon so heavily, tax-deferred annuities and, as Walt said, non-qualified deferred comp plans and regular brokerage accounts.

Walt: As our clients move through our planning process, we determine a long-term goal of building funds for retirement. This is certainly not one-size-fits-all, as each client has different assets and different needs. If you have a lot of disposable income when you are investing money into a qualified retirement plan (for instance, $800,000 in annual income), your income tax rate may be pretty much the same during retirement as it is during your working career.

Qualified retirement plans, like a 401(k), are set up with the understanding that during your working life, when you are funding those plans, you will be in the highest tax bracket. Those plans are designed for you to take a deduction when you are in a potentially high tax bracket, and when you receive your retirement funds, it is supposed to be at a lower tax rate.

As we discussed earlier in the book, with our country's history of fluctuating tax rates, that might not hold right now. Think about all the money the federal government recently spent in attempts to combat the coronavirus pandemic, as well as funds provided to individuals whose livelihoods and businesses were damaged. Therefore, you could be in a *higher* tax bracket upon retirement because of COVID-19 or other unforeseen disasters. This is what we worry about when it comes to qualified retire-

> "THE 401(K) WAS NEVER MEANT TO BE THE CENTERPIECE OF ANYONE'S RETIREMENT."
>
> TODD MARDIS

ment plans. Congress could suddenly vote to set the tax rate at 100% if they felt strongly about it, and the President could sign it into law. While something *that* extreme is unlikely, we are cautious about qualified retirement plans because tax rates have been very high at times. Those plans have a place in the mix, but we do not see them as the primary funding vehicle for retirement.

Todd: Congress passed the Revenue Act of 1978, which included Section 401(k). By 1982 businesses had begun offering them to employees as one of the perks of employment. The 401(k) was a way for those individuals to save additional dollars on top of other retirement benefits like pension plans. These were never meant to be the centerpiece of anyone's retirement. Interestingly, only 13% of today's businesses offer pension plans compared to 40% in 1979. As Walt said, the 401(k) has morphed into something it was not meant to be - it was never meant to be your only source of retirement income.

To really drive this point home, let's say I offer you a $100,000 loan. You will want to know when to pay it back and the interest rate. What if I were to tell you we would decide the interest rate later? Would you take the $100,000? Who would take out a loan with no clear idea of what the interest rate would be well down the road?

This is how the 401(k) program works. You take the tax deduction today, but you are unsure of the future tax rates or what you will be charged when you begin distributing those funds. A 401(k) does not really allow you to take a tax deduction - it's a tax deferral. Investing $100,000 in a 401(k) is not saving you $50,000 in taxes; it may have, instead, *deferred* $75,000 in taxes.

Furthermore, when a successful business owner with a higher level of income retires, he will still accrue income. That can really hurt from a tax perspective. First, 401(k) distributions are taxed as ordinary income. Because these types of people have been successful, they are able to invest more money into their retirement, so there is more money to distribute. Thus, the more they distribute, the higher the marginal rates.

Beyond that, once they retire, the first thing they lose is their business deductions. Business deductions are beautiful things - maybe they are writing off car payments, phone bills, and health insurance. They could take all these deductions as a business owner. However, when they retire and sell their business, those deductions diminish, and their taxable income increases. People in this position may also accumulate multiple sources of income. Maybe they sell their business and begin receiving installment payments from the purchaser. They might have rental income as well. So there is still a lot of income coming in, and they are drawing out of 401(k) funds that have not been taxed. Compound it with what we discussed earlier in the book about the historically low marginal tax rates: the top rate may become mid to low-range over the next 10-20 years because of all the spending. With this in mind, when you distribute money from the 401(k), you might be taxed at a *higher* rate than you were when you invested it.

Walt: Many of our clients are physicians who pay off their homes, purchase a beachfront condo, and load up their 401(k) thinking they are set for life. Nevertheless, what happens if you are one year from retirement and Congress decides to tax your 401(k) distributions at 70%? Suddenly, your share of the $2 million sitting in your IRA is $600,000. That conversation has been difficult for many of our clients. They never really considered that a massive tax increase can claim a significant portion of their retirement in one fell swoop. As you review your retirement plan, review strategies that would allow you to take money out of the 401(k) at the current rate, as they are fairly low.

Todd: We touched on the other problems with IRAs in previous chapters as well. Recall how the SECURE Act (The Setting Every Community Up For Retirement Enhancement Act) killed the ability to take IRAs you inherit and keep them for an extended period of time *without* having to pay taxes or take distributions.

Walt: We also mentioned the government has been looking at retirement plans as a form of social capital. Congress has taxed excessive distributions on qualified retirement plans to the tune of 10-15%. In effect, they penalized people for funding their retirement plans too much. While those excess taxes were repealed and the use of qualified retirement plans as social capital has been just hearsay until this point, that demonstrates how legislative action can quickly take a big bite out of years of saving for retirement.

Todd: As of this writing, there is over $10 trillion in 401(k) plans and defined benefit plans, and our federal government spends about $100 billion on them each year. So yes, the IRS, governors, and elected officials in Washington know those funds are there. Furthermore, they also know there are ways to access those funds through legislation. Sooner or later, there is a good chance they are coming after qualified retirement money in some form or fashion.

Hence, a 401(k) by itself might not be your best retirement option. Keep in mind, there are three eroding factors to all investments:

1) Taxes
2) Market Corrections

3) Expenses

Your 401(k) is an example of *all* three. They can be wonderful strategies to *help* fund retirement, but it would not be very reasonable to build one's entire retirement around it.

Walt: Therefore, we recommend a well-rounded retirement portfolio. For instance, another source of retirement funding can be real estate investments. Many of our clients own real estate or rental properties. There can be a decent appreciation in tax benefits in owning the property where your business sits. There are distributions to the client that can be tax-free as the depreciation and other expenses cover those taxes.

We encourage our clients early in their professional careers to own their own real estate. Sometimes there are legitimate reasons not to, such as the placement of one's business in their city. Still, about 90% of our clients own real estate. It becomes a cash source during retirement because when they ultimately sell out to the next generation in the business succession plan, they typically keep the real estate and receive the cash from it in the form of rental income. Those transactions typically involve holding the real estate for a period of time to receive income and then selling the building to the new business owner.

Todd: Real estate investments have a couple of benefits. Not only do you have the potential for residual rental income after you sell your business, but a business sale that also includes real estate is much more attractive to a buyer than buying a business that is housed on someone else's real estate. The only caveat is most of the income is passive, which is difficult to offset unless you retain passive losses. Other than that, this strategy is very effective and something you should be working toward if you are a business owner.

Anyone who owns a business should have a succession plan in place, regardless. When it is time for retirement, look to extract value from all your years of hard work. Selling a business can be challenging, so be sure to plan years in advance. When a few of our clients were ready to sell their business, they identified the buyer they would like to work with. Unfortunately, the buyer, at times, encounters problems accessing the capital to purchase the company. There might be terms the buyer cannot or will not agree to. The transaction itself can be very inefficient from a tax standpoint as well. For instance, when the buyer purchases the business with after-tax dollars, they must earn $1.40 to generate a dollar to spend on the transaction. As the seller, you must report that same dollar as a capital gain or income. This depends on how the transaction is structured, meaning the same dollar is taxed both to the buyer and the seller.

A tax attorney like Walt can help mitigate some of the sale's taxes by structuring it properly. Other techniques can enable you to receive a premium on the sale of your business. The main point is your business can be one of the most important assets in your retirement portfolio.

Another form of retirement is utilizing an annuity. Annuities can be funded through index options, where your returns are based on the returns of the S&P 500 less dividends. You can invest in equities in the market, or your insurance company can pay you a fixed, guaranteed rate predetermined before you purchase an annuity. Annuities vary in length from three, five, seven, and up to ten years.

One thing people love about annuities is they avoid probate, so they are simple to administer. They are a lot like life insurance: you designate a beneficiary, and if you pass away, your beneficiary receives the value of the annuity. If you set up a ten-

RETIREMENT INVESTMENTS AND EROSION

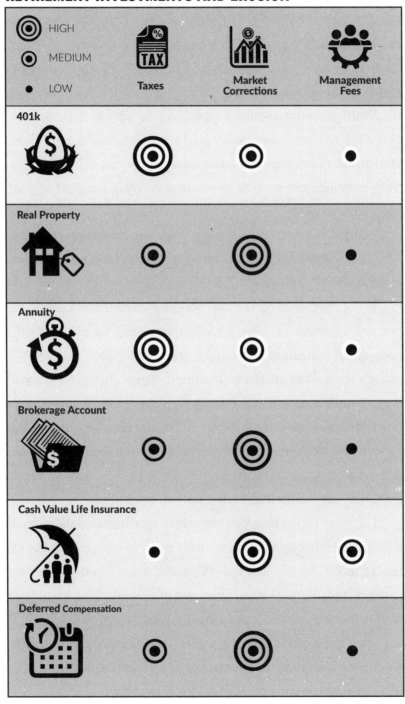

	Taxes	Market Corrections	Management Fees
Legend: HIGH / MEDIUM / LOW			
401k	HIGH	MEDIUM	LOW
Real Property	MEDIUM	HIGH	LOW
Annuity	HIGH	MEDIUM	LOW
Brokerage Account	MEDIUM	HIGH	LOW
Cash Value Life Insurance	LOW	HIGH	MEDIUM
Deferred Compensation	MEDIUM	HIGH	LOW

year annuity, for example, and die in the second year, your beneficiary would receive another eight years of distribution. You can structure the benefits from an annuity to insulate them from market corrections, which is a big positive for many investors. They also grow on a tax-deferred basis, so the interest grows inside the annuity each year.

Walt: In some annuities, you have an option to receive income for life, and companies will calculate the benefit. Those tend to be more expensive because the contracts last so long. Still, annuities can provide you with security in terms of regular, long-term income.

Todd: Like with any strategy, there are downsides to annuities. They generate a tax, so the distributions would be subject to taxation.

Walt: Annuities can be complex, so you need to know what you are investing in. They are contract-based, which means the companies that manage them are very concerned with technicalities in the way they are structured. They often have a lot of leeway in how they manage them for you.

Todd: The last annuity I owned was in a brokerage account. Essentially, brokerage accounts hold investment equities that can be used for retirement income. Though they may be fun to own, they are inefficient from a tax standpoint.

The main problem is you are investing after-tax dollars. Your investment must do well right away, even to earn back your after-tax money, much less the before-tax money you had to earn to deposit the funds. Unless you hold onto your gains for at least twelve months, you will pay ordinary income tax on the gains. If you want to pay the long-term capital gain rate instead, you must hold those positions for over a year, which can be tough to do if you trade inside your account on a routine basis.

In essence, you are investing money that has been taxed, paying ordinary income tax on the gains, then still dealing with fees and market corrections on top of those taxes for high net-worth individuals who are in a high marginal bracket. Again, brokerage accounts are fun but not very efficient from a tax perspective and certainly are not something our clients typically use as the main source of retirement income.

Walt: From an estate planning perspective, you can pass on income tax benefits to your heirs if you use living brokerage accounts that have appreciation to the next generation. This is known as a "stepped-up" basis. As an extreme example, if you own a stock in a brokerage account that you purchased for $1,000 and a generation later it grows to $10 million, the beneficiary can sell all of it for absolutely no capital gains or ordinary income taxes after the original holder has passed away. Brokerage accounts may not be a good retirement strategy, but to Todd's point, these can be fun accounts if you inherit them.

Todd: Another retirement strategy is utilizing cash value life insurance. Cash value life insurance policies get a bad rap from those who think they are bad investments. When you research, you will find these have impeccable tax benefits. Those policies can play a very strategic role in one's retirement years for several reasons.

Cash value policies insulate you from market corrections. You may not earn as much in a cash value life scenario every year, but you will probably keep more because your money's value has not decreased. From a tax perspective, the money goes into the policy as after-tax dollars, but unlike a brokerage account or even a 401(k), the money grows and, if set up properly, can be pulled out tax-free.

This is very important if you are in tune with what you *keep*

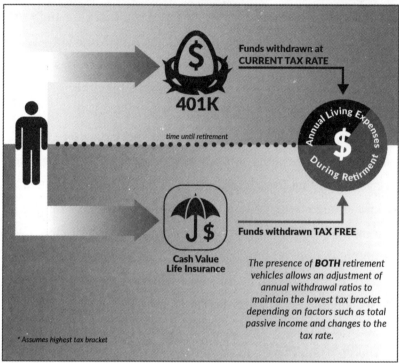

vs. what you *earn*. I might have a million dollars in a 401(k), but ultimately, it may be worth about $650,000 after paying taxes. If I have a million dollars in a cash-value life insurance policy, I can receive the distributions *tax-free*.

Cash-value life insurance policies also insulate you from fees. In any 401(k) or brokerage account, your fees increase based on the amount of volume in your account. Say you pay 1.5% in fees for your brokerage account or your 401(k). That is about $1,500 per year for an account containing $100,000, or $15,000 per year for a million-dollar account. There is a large upfront fee for cash-value life insurance policies that the life insurance company pays the broker. However, after the fees are paid, there are very minimal renewal fees. They are usually from

1.5 - 2.0% from years 2-10, so it is comparable to a brokerage account or 401(k). However, those fees discontinue after year ten, and the fees to your brokerage or 401(k) account remain. The fees paid in a brokerage account or 401(k) are roughly 4-5 times as much as those paid in a cash-value life insurance scenario.

As you can see, a cash-value life insurance policy is a valuable tool for mitigating taxes. If you are withdrawing from a 401(k), you cannot control the tax bracket and could be paying more in taxes as you withdraw your funds. If you own a cash-value life insurance policy, you can mitigate your taxes by withdrawing just enough from your 401(k) to stay within a certain tax bracket. You then withdraw the remainder of what you need from your cash-value life insurance.

Life insurance allows you to play offense from a tax perspective even in your retirement years, and it is a precious asset.

Walt: One of the benefits of life insurance is borrowing tax-free funds from the policy. Distributions can be taken out as loans and can be paid back with the insured's death benefit. That represents a huge advantage over a 401(k), which might be taxed at the highest marginal rate. This is a key component, making life insurance a superior funding vehicle for our non-qualified deferred compensation plan.

A non-qualified deferred comp plan works in a similar plan as the cash-value life insurance. Still, it has one additional characteristic: it uses a lower tax structure because it allows the creation of a C Corporation. After the Trump tax bill, the C Corporation now has a 21% tax bracket, instead of 15% and 25%.

Reviewing the difference between the 21% in the C Corporation and the 37% rate an individual in the highest bracket would experience, that is a significant difference of 16%. If you

NON-QUALIFIED DEFERRED COMPENSATION BENEFIT OF A C-CORP

consider this tax differential on, say, $100,000, you are saving $16,000 on the contribution through a C Corporation compared to depositing money into investment funds.

Not only are you saving money when you invest in the plan, but you will also be able to borrow from the policy tax-free for the rest of your life and not have to pay it back. When you pass, the insurance proceeds will pay off the loan. Your beneficiary receives whatever is left in the policy.

Todd: Deferred comp plans are great tools. Of course, we do not believe any assets are individually superior nor should be used in exclusivity. All can be used in conjunction with each other to create a more efficient retirement plan.

Walt: Now that we gave you an overview of the different strategies you can use to develop a more efficient retirement plan, we will focus on one of those strategies in particular - your business. Your business can be used to create excellent strategies for retirement. In the next chapter, we will review approaches for creating tax deductions with your business.

KEY TAKEAWAYS

Retirement strategies are not a one size fits all solution. Strategies must be tailored to the individual circumstances, and typically a combination of strategies is required to achieve the desired results.

The relative success of a 401k is largely tied to the actual rate of taxation when you draw your funds out during retirement. Because future tax rates cannot be known with any certainty, a 401k should typically not be relied upon as a primary retirement strategy.

Each retirement investment should be evaluated, in part by its susceptibility to the three erosion factors: taxes, market correction, and management expenses.

Cash value life insurance policies are a good example of an investment strategy that stands strong against erosion factors. Such policies are not subject to taxes upon withdrawal, not subject to market corrections, and have management expenses that decrease over time.

Certain corporate structures can create retirement strategy opportunities not otherwise available (i.e. a non-qualified deferred compensation plan within a C Corporation). An experienced tax attorney should be utilized to evaluate the opportunity, and to execute the formation of, such structures.

VIDEO RESOURCES

LINK: bit.ly/Crusaders11

LINK: bit.ly/Crusaders25

LINK: bit.ly/Crusaders26

JAMES MADISON

"ARMIES, DEBTS, AND TAXES
ARE THE KNOWN INSTRUMENTS
FOR BRINGING THE MANY
UNDER THE DOMINATION
OF THE FEW."

USING YOUR BUSINESS FOR TAX BENEFITS

Walt: Many people overlook tax deductions they could take advantage of, and we believe the reason comes down to a lack of education. When our clients approach us, they often do not realize what is available to them and allowed by the law, much less how to create a proper financial plan.

Todd: Remember, the U.S. Tax Code is roughly 2,600 pages. Obviously, it is an enormous document, and we do not expect taxpayers to know the Tax Code from cover to cover. Interestingly, of those 2,600 pages, *approximately 80% of them are dedicated to how to use your business to take deductions.* That is well over 2,000 pages of possible deductions! The document is so vast one person or firm cannot totally understand all 2,600 pages. Thus, this is where we often see overlooked deductions.

Walt: If you do not take all the deductions your business is entitled to, you usually do not have a sound overall plan on the front end. Having a sound plan that fits everything together is essential so your deductions make reasonable sense. Advanced planning is important, and the lack of it is one of the biggest mistakes we encounter. It is imperative to understand the criteria for the deduction. It can mean the difference between having a deduction accepted or denied.

For example, sometimes, we create a family entity that utilizes members of the family like employees. Your typical family vacation to Disney World ordinarily is not deductible. Still, if you have just the right set of facts and the trip is for the benefit of that entity's employees, a deduction can be available for the whole crew. Travel costs, food, and other expenses can be 100% deductible. It is all explained under Section 162 of the Tax Code. The main consideration is the ordinary and necessary test. Is it ordinary in terms of fair market value, and is it helpful to the business? There must be a connection to the business, and the trip must be helpful to it. Of course, the IRS may not like the deduction very much if the only people going on the trip are family members, so this is something you will need to weigh and do a cost/benefit analysis.

Another example along the same lines is an individual who has a corporation, and their spouse and children are all employees. They visit Disney World for several days and plan to have a wonderful time exploring and sightseeing. Todd and I also visit and schedule a block of four hours to work on a marketing plan. In that case, if they can show it was for the corporation's primary benefit and document the four-hour block of time working on the marketing plan, the individual can deduct 100% of the trip

THE "ORDINARY AND NECESSARY" TEST BASED ON SECTION 162 OF THE TAX CODE

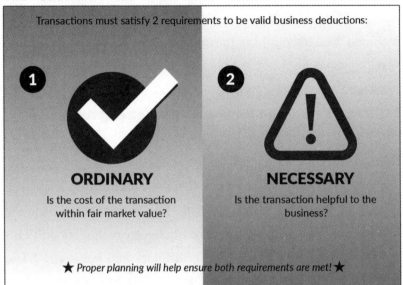

Transactions must satisfy 2 requirements to be valid business deductions:

1

ORDINARY

Is the cost of the transaction within fair market value?

2

NECESSARY

Is the transaction helpful to the business?

★ *Proper planning will help ensure both requirements are met!* ★

as employee entertainment. To take the deduction and pass the IRS test, they would need to show how the trip benefitted what the family performs as a company.

Todd: You cannot merely purchase tickets to Disney World, write them off, and expect the deduction. It would be best to have meticulous and thorough documentation of the marketing session and travel, meals, and lodging. Perhaps the big reason for the trip is morale, and a beloved employee passed away. Everyone is struggling to cope with the loss. If the employee who passed away was highly involved in the company's marketing, it might be ideal for taking a comprehensive look at what the marketing plans would look like moving forward.

While on the trip, you could also participate in other activities. For example, if you wanted to offer a fishing outing for your employees while your company is at Disney World, you could deduct those expenses as well. If the food on the fishing trip, the gasoline, and the captain who pilots the boat add up to a total cost of $2,500, we could deduct 100% of the fishing trip because all the company employees - not just a select few - were included. The overarching reason, which included the marketing session, was a big morale-booster for the company.

There was a case where an employer rented a yacht for $4,100 a day. Because there were many employees, and to ensure everyone participated, the yacht was taken out five separate times. He took a deduction under Section 162 for the expense. The employer was able to show there was noticeably-improved morale at the office after the trip. The employees developed bonds, and relationships improved between managers and employees. Ultimately, was this trip ordinary and necessary? The court agreed it was. It was more than a mere fun excursion. The business was able to show the court a tangible benefit from taking everyone on an expensive yachting trip.

Todd: As a business owner, you treat seven employees and take them to Atlantic City. You plan to study and discuss your production. Yet, admittedly, you spend most of your time partying, gambling, going to dinners, and having cocktails. You stay for two nights then return to the office. Would that be deductible?

If you categorize the event as recreational for your employees, then it *would* be tax-deductible. If you do not, then the only things you performed in your business would be worth a 50% deduction. Certain tests must be met when declaring the trip as a recreational event; you do not discriminate or define by salary, such as treating people who only make more than $110,000 annually. You must also take 80% of all employees, and there must be a W-2 relationship in place. This does not work with 1099 strategic partners or contract employees. The business must employ the person for whom the deduction is made.

If you meet all criteria, you may deduct costs associated with transportation, meals, and lodging for your employees. This is much better than only taking half of some expenses, which will be the case if the Atlantic City junket is not listed as recreational. The IRS wants this threshold to be met because the recreation must benefit the rank and file more than it benefits the owner and the highly-compensated employees.

The great thing about employee entertainment is that it is 100% deductible including holiday parties, annual picnics, and summer outings. Your employees can attend Christmas parties, even Super Bowl parties. You can maintain a swimming pool, baseball diamond, bowling alley, golf course - these are examples given to us by the IRS.

Walt and I completely understand how this might seem very illogical. The idea of deducting 100% of the meal costs on a fun trip, when you can only deduct 50% for heavy-duty business meetings, might seem wrong. Yet this is how lawmakers in Washington organized it, and it is a rule we apply to benefit our clients.

Walt: We mentioned in an earlier chapter one of our clients who owned a ski lodge in Colorado that he unsuccessfully attempted to sell. He spoke to his CPA about it, and the CPA advised him to hold the lodge as rental property so he could write

> ## "LACK OF PLANNING IS ONE OF THE BIGGEST MISTAKES WE SEE."
>
> WALT DALLAS

off his expenses. Our client was unsure about the idea, but the CPA promised him it would work, and he took the deductions.

Sure enough, the IRS audited him. They asked all kinds of

questions about the ski lodge: Had he ever dealt with a broker to manage it for him? Had he placed ads in a local newspaper to advertise it? Did he have any contracts with any third parties? The answer to all those questions was no, and the deduction was denied. The deduction could have been effective if he and his then-CPA had created a plan upfront. They could have had documentation in place and taken depreciation deductions, and there would have been a sound case in favor of the deduction - even if the lodge were left unrented. If it *had* been rented, even a time or two, that is an even better set of facts.

Todd: What about writing off expenses related to your home? Tax code Section 280A has been in existence since the Eisenhower administration. In the 1980s it was recodified and became Section 280A(g). This code allows you to rent your home up to *fourteen* times on a tax-free basis. Our clients use their homes for legitimate business meetings, and it can create a nice tax deduction for the corporation and tax-free income for the client.

For example, an endodontist hosts a monthly staff meeting at his home. At the meeting they review procedures, issues with human resources, how well their accounts receivables are being paid, which carriers they are having issues with, and how they can streamline processes. The monthly meeting provides a lot of tangible benefits to the practice.

We see this as being especially beneficial when the client does not have a meeting facility large enough to gather the whole team into one location. Typically, dental offices are not large enough for everyone to meet in one room. There are greeting spaces, labs, and exam rooms. As patients are routinely scheduled for all hours of each day, these spaces are always in use. Essentially, it is nearly impossible for one or more reasons to have a much-needed meeting on site. A scheduled Saturday morning meeting with food provided at the endodontist's home makes an atmosphere possible where work can be maximized without interruption. That more than justifies the deduction.

Walt: The time on Saturday morning and the food would be listed as an expense. If it is a recurring monthly meeting, multiply the time block and food by twelve.

Todd: Over the course of a year, that could create a deduction of $15,000-$20,000 depending on the home's value. Some would argue you could just as easily find a hotel meeting room. Still, you might be in an area that does not have readily available space - you might not want to ask your employees to drive half an hour one way to find a hotel across the city when your home might be just a few minutes from your office.

Walt: Were this to progress to appeals against the IRS, you would need to be ready to prove the home meetings are ordinary and reasonable. Is it helpful to the business? In the example of the dentist hosting staff meetings at his home, I would say so for all the reasons we discussed.

Todd: It is important to point out in this scenario that you need to have a thoroughly documented system for how you calculate the rental amount. The figure you charge for the block of time each month to use your home as a meeting site needs to be attained through a third-party appraisal and not simply a number you estimate on your own.

Walt: Code Section 119 allows employees to have meals called "Meals for the Convenience of the Employer." As part of the COVID-19 Economic Relief Bill, business meals from a restaurant are 100% deductible. Meals need to be on the employer's business premises and for the employer's convenience, such as if the employer needs the employee to perform certain functions during the lunch hour. If the meals are what you would normally eat (nothing extravagant), they can be a valid deduction as they benefit the employer.

Todd: If properly structured under Section 105, there are ways to deduct out-of-pocket medical costs, excluding over-the-counter medications and cosmetic expenses for you and/or your dependents. Medical costs refer to pharmaceutical, dental, and optometric costs. Those are only deductible under some corporate structures if they exceed 7.5% of the company's gross annual income. Reaching this threshold may be out of reach if you are earning $800,000 a year. Frankly, we tell clients we hope they never qualify for receiving this deduction with a high-income level.

On average, we see families of five spending anywhere from $3,000-$5,000 a year on out-of-pocket medical costs, including co-pays, deductibles, prescription refills, and more. If you have a child who needs braces, you will spend roughly $6,000. If your corporate structure is set up to include them as employees who receive compensation and perform services for the corporation, this is a 100% deductible expense from dollar one under a medical reimbursement plan.

Walt: If I am an employee, but my son is a non-employee, I can still use medical reimbursement as a deduction.

Todd: When you have a newborn, you accrue multiple out-of-pocket expenses: OBGYN, prenatal visits, anesthesiologists, hospital stay, and medications. Under the Code, they become a 100% tax-deductible expense for the corporation.

Walt: Disability insurance coverage is another deduction to consider. Many of our clients are professionals: doctors, dentists, attorneys. It is essential they own top-notch disability contracts. In those contracts, we recommend they are set up as occupation-specific, meaning if they cannot work in their chosen occupation, they are considered disabled—*even if they can work in a different occupation.*

This is important, for example, for surgeons who might lose dexterity in the hands and are no longer able to practice. The surgeon could still be extremely productive teaching at a medical school or dental school. He could serve as a consultant for a company that develops medical devices or enter a completely new line of work, like selling real estate. Still, under the disability contract, the individual would be considered disabled if the contract is set up in the beginning as occupation-specific. With proper disability coverage, those outside earnings from different occupations do not offset their monthly disability benefits.

As you can imagine, those policies become very expensive. We see the premiums ranging from $5,000-$15,000 per year. CPS clients enjoy an approximate 40% discount because of how we structured the reimbursement of disability premiums. We created a deduction and a tax-free reimbursement to the employees. Again, this must be completed properly. If not, you can trigger taxation of benefits if the individual becomes disabled.

Todd: For example, an individual earns $250,000 per year and pays $14,000 for disability premiums. In a tax bracket of 35%, that is around $75,000 in taxes. Normally, he would need

> "WE ALWAYS USE TAX ATTORNEYS WHEN PUTTING THESE PLANS TOGETHER. THESE ARE VERY UNIQUE STRATEGIES THAT REQUIRE WHAT WE DESCRIBE AS 'GOOD FACT PATTERNS.'"
>
> TODD MARDIS

to earn about $23,000 to pay a $14,000 premium to the insurance company with after-tax earnings.

On the other hand, in that example, CPS clients have a net cost of about $8,400 by having the right structure and a better way to pay their disability premiums.

We always use tax attorneys when organizing these plans. These are unique strategies that require what we describe as "good fact patterns." Everything must be outlined carefully. As we say, good facts fit the U.S. Tax Code. If they do not fit the Code and you face an audit, you will not receive the deductions.

Walt: We cannot stress enough the importance of having knowledgeable tax professionals working with you. Without them, you can miss deductions you should be taking advantage of or, worse, taking deductions in a way the IRS will not accept. In fact, in the next chapter, we will cover some common mistakes we see and how you can keep from making those mistakes.

KEY TAKEAWAYS

Approximately 80% of the US tax code is dedicated to explaining how deductions can be made through business entities.

Many business deductions are defined by Section 162 of the Tax Code, which puts forth the "Ordinary and Necessary Test." In other words, is the expense ordinary in terms of fair market expense, and is it helpful to the business?

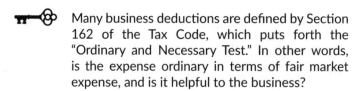

Knowing the specific requirements for a deduction in advance allows you to conform your actions to the letter of the law so that fact patterns are squarely in your favor and the deduction will withstand scrutiny.

▶ VIDEO RESOURCES

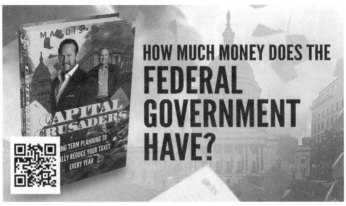

LINK: bit.ly/Crusaders12

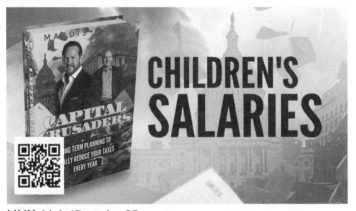

LINK: bit.ly/Crusaders27

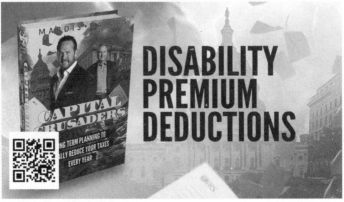

LINK: bit.ly/Crusaders28

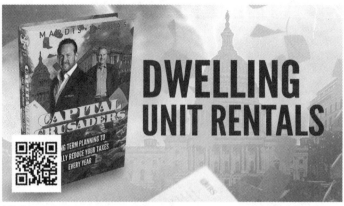

LINK: bit.ly/Crusaders29

LINK: bit.ly/Crusaders30

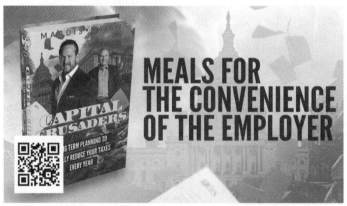

LINK: bit.ly/Crusaders31

THOMAS PAINE

"TAXES ARE NOT RAISED TO
CARRY ON WARS, BUT RATHER
WARS ARE RAISED TO
CARRY ON TAXES."

COMMON MISTAKES

Todd: With a system as complicated as our tax system, we frequently witness people making mistakes that cost them a lot of money. You would probably be surprised to learn even good businesspeople make simple and easily-fixable tax mistakes. While we certainly see businesses making unusual mistakes, for the most part the problems they have are the same problems many other businesses have encountered. We wanted to spend a little time outlining the most common issues, hoping you will not make these mistakes as you begin developing your tax strategy.

Walt: Even people who do a great job running their company either do not understand their business's tax side or rely on their CPAs to save them tax money. As we said before, that's really not the CPA's job.

Todd: One of the most common problems we see is a business simply growing in size without growing in sophistication. When that happens, you see people earning $400,000-$500,000 still being taxed as a sole proprietorship. There are several problems with a Sole Proprietorship at that level of income. First, as we mentioned, it is a higher audit risk. Secondly, there more deductions and efficiencies available to businesses inside an LLC, S Corporation election.

Walt: By not properly structuring your business, you may be paying way too much in payroll taxes. We see clients earning over a million dollars and quite commonly paying an extra 3.8% on $800,000 of their income.

Todd: Beyond that, we often see people who do have the correct corporate structure but do not know how to utilize it efficiently. We see this particularly with S Corporations, where the IRS requires you to pay yourself a reasonable salary. Business owners might pay themselves extremely high salaries, which means they are overpaying payroll taxes. CPS has third-party studies performed in those instances to determine what would be considered reasonable. This safeguards our clients to set their salary at a reasonable level without overpaying on payroll taxes.

Walt: We have a client who earns in excess of $800,000 annually. His CPA told him to form an S Corporation and pay himself a salary. This would have been a good recommendation had the client not paid the full 800,000 in salary but taken a reasonable salary and the remaining income in distributions. After engaging CPS we moved his salary to $200,000 and took $600,000 in distributions. This resulted in an ongoing tax savings of $21,000 a year.

Todd: That's an example of a CPA being very busy and not taking the time to look at each client on an individual basis, as $21,000 is significant. Calculate this amount each year for a decade, and it is *very* significant.

Walt: As we discussed in Chapter Five, another mistake would be the failure to record substantiation at or near the event's time. As soon as possible - preferably right then - provides a high-credibility level at the appeals level. As we mentioned before, many people stick their receipts in a shoebox with the intention to revisit it later, and this approach has much less value.

We mentioned before the complaints our CPA friends have about their clients' recordkeeping. That is why we developed the Document Assistance Program to address this problem. We train our clients to document anything associated with a possible deduction right away. It is as simple as taking a photo with their phone - we teach them a system within their phone, allowing them to save the receipt on the spot. That way, it is available permanently, and they will not need to search for it later. Your plan should include a recordkeeping system that explains what kind of documents to keep, how to prepare, organize, and maintain them efficiently. It is wise to include a category for employee entertainment in your recordkeeping in the same way you include meals and travel.

Todd: While the receipt is a great first step, having business purpose notes on the receipt is the number one area where we see mistakes. You might file a receipt that may or may not be business-related, but you do not document *how* it was related or how it might be a deductible business expense after time passes.

Remember, the IRS cannot disprove something you can prove, but they can certainly deny something you *cannot* prove. If I take my wife out to dinner and take the deduction, it may or may not be challenged. Still, if my spouse works inside the business and we go out, I could write up a short draft of all the things we discuss from a business planning perspective and take a legitimate deduction.

Developing the habit of noting the substantiation and having a great recording system is a big step. We see many people who create a structure for keeping records and still adhere to it five, ten, even twenty years later.

I will add, though, while we work carefully with our clients to retain a substantiation structure and recordkeeping strengths, even the best plans can become inefficient as the Tax Code evolves. It is important to update as needed. If someone purchases a created business in 1982, the purchaser must know corporate structures from 1982 are *much* different today in 2021. Many times, business owners maintain the same structure they had when purchasing the business. That does not always work.

Walt: That's one more reason regular reevaluation of the substantiation structure is required. Updating your plan is crucial.

We frequently see another issue with people storing all their retirement eggs in one basket while building up a substantial qualified-plan balance. Again, we do not know what the tax rate will be in the future. Congress and the President could agree on some mind-boggling tax rate, 98%, perhaps. That has happened in the past. Everything you save for retirement will be used to pay taxes. We do not like to see a retirement plan built around one single element that could fall apart and derail a lifetime of dreams and planning. As Todd and I have both said, a 401(k) is popular and is a good start. Still, your retirement should have multiple strategies in place.

Todd: In addition to our country's history concerning 401(k)s, the plan costs you might not even consider can make them an inefficient choice for employers. If you are an employer and you have a qualified 401(k) plan, there are certain rules you must adhere to. The maximum contribution level for an employer this year is $57,000 - any additional contributions must flow to the employees' benefits. If you want to be able to invest the $57,000 into your qualified retirement account, the IRS requires employers to contribute money to their employees whether those employees want to contribute to the plan or not.

In 2017, the maximum contribution level for the employer's benefit was $54,000. The remaining contributions had to flow to the employees' benefits. At the time, a client of ours owned a law practice with nine employees. If he invested $110,000 into retirement, only $54,000 could go to benefit the employer. The remaining $56,000 went to the employees. That is almost counterproductive - they were essentially spending $100 to save $50. Would it make more sense for the employer to give his employees a raise rather than contribute to their 401(k)? In this case, we suggested the employer continue with a traditional 401(k) for himself, which allowed him to invest $19,000 a year into his own retirement, and then give his employees a $2,000 raise.

Instead of spending an extra $56,000 to have $18,000 in tax savings, he could invest those funds into an alternative investment account. The attorney now has nearly $78,000 to invest in his retirement for the same out-of-pocket costs. His employees are also happy because of the $2,000 annual raise while still enjoying the ability to fund their 401(k) plans.

I asked numerous clients how much they spend on employee contributions. The number one response: "I have no idea." The 401(k) is definitely not a set-it-on-the-shelf plan - it's something you must watch carefully. It goes back to what was discussed with a corporate structure: these individuals may have started their 401(k) and profit-sharing plan when they had three em-

COMMON MISTAKES WE SEE CLIENTS MAKE

Outgrowth of Corporate Structure

The proper corporate structure for your business operation is based on numerous factors. The correct choice for the first few years of operation may be rendered obsolete through years of growth and expansion.

Overpayment of Payroll Taxes

High income earners commonly fall into a trap that results in overpayment of income taxes by 3.8%! Avoid this mistake through proper planning.

Inefficient Use of Proper Corporate Structure

Different corporate structures operate by different rules. Even when you are operating in the proper structure for your current business dynamic, you must be aware of the rules that apply to your structure so you can maximize the benefits.

Failure to Record Substantiation at Time of the Event

We are all victims of diminishing memory and faded receipts. A good system of recordkeeping at the time of the deductable transaction prevents both problems and is evidence of a business owner who is serious about conducting business in accordance with the tax code.

Failure to Regularly Update Tax Strategy

The United States tax code is constantly changing. New provisions, or elimination of old ones, can drastically impact your operation and render obsolete previously sound strategies. Stay diligent!

Building Retirement Strategies Around a Single Technique

The effectiveness of every retirement technique is subject to future events that can not be predicted with 100% certainty. Your best bet is to enter retirement with multiple investment vehicles in play to provide maximum flexibility to react to the unexpected.

Incorrect Corporate Structure at Time of Retirement

The proper corporate structure for your business operation will likely change over the years due to factors such as growth and changes to the tax code. Easy to overlook is the fact that your retirement strategy can also have a significant impact on which structure you need when you decide to call it a career.

ployees. It may have been a great safe-harbor then, but not so much today with thirty employees.

Walt: Another common mistake with qualified plans is not thinking through the right structure that should be in place at retirement. Even if rates stay the same, if you withdraw at the same rate as you deposit, you have not accomplished anything other than paying a bunch of 401(k) fees.

Some of our clients invested in 401(k)s when George W. Bush was President and the tax rate was 35%. If they withdraw now, they will be taxed at the maximum rate of 37%. They are actually paying more than they would have paid at the time of the contribution. As Todd mentioned, you should be thinking about what will happen upon withdrawal and long-term gain when considering a 401(k).

Todd: Sometimes, things make perfect sense when you do them. Still, as you grow and change, or as the rules change, those same things do not make sense anymore. Business owners should continually review the different components of their day-to-day business. That starts with corporate structure and employee benefits - research what deductions may be available today that were not available when you started your business. If I start a business and have one employee - or none - I need to label myself as a sole proprietor. I might not earn enough to have payroll tax issues, and I do not pay out enough to justify another $12,000 to have a separate tax return filed.

A sole proprietorship might be the perfect structure for me in the beginning. In a few years though, I will have six employees. My income will have soared from an initial $30,000 a year to $430,000. The structure that worked perfectly well in the beginning would no longer work. If you are using an initial structure to fund your company's 401(k) benefits and your business has seen the kind of growth I just mentioned, you are most likely getting killed by the costs of paying out 401(k) benefits.

Walt: We hope this review has helped you understand what to avoid as you design your own tax savings strategy. Some of the concepts we laid out in this book may seem fairly simple; others are very complicated, and we wouldn't recommend trying them on your own. In the next chapter, we will give you a preview of our review process at CPS to see what goes into planning a tax savings strategy.

⑪ KEY TAKEAWAYS

Tax saving strategies must be reevaluated over time. A sound strategy today may be rendered obsolete through even positive developments, such as the growth of your business.

Documentation and substantiation is vital to any tax savings strategy. The system you implement must be easy enough to maintain that it can be, and is, executed at all times.

▶ VIDEO RESOURCES

LINK: bit.ly/Crusaders13

LINK: bit.ly/Crusaders32

FRANKLIN D. ROOSEVELT

"TAXES, AFTER ALL, ARE DUES
THAT WE PAY FOR THE PRIVILEGES OF
MEMBERSHIP IN AN ORGANIZED SOCIETY."

A REVIEW OF YOUR CURRENT SITUATION

Todd: Working with CPS is a straightforward process. First, we gather basic data. We provide our clients with a short questionnaire that requests items like marital status, number of children, whether those kids are in public or private schools, or even college. We ask how much our clients spend on certain things, such as out-of-pocket medical costs or investments. We inquire about their current financial capacity, a general state of mind regarding investing, and what they anticipate their income to be in the coming year. We obtain the client's most recent tax filings, both individual and business. We usually review the last two years of returns if possible, which indicates whether the client's business has trended up or down. Sometimes clients have, for instance, borrowed money to expand their business. Things of this nature can have a significant impact on net revenue as we advance. This allows us to customize a plan rather than proposing generic recommendations.

Walt: Once we receive the information, we begin our planning process. We evaluate the data to determine available tax savings based on the clients' structures. We then compare that to tax savings available if we implement new or different structures and add strategies they are not currently employing. A tax attorney has designed the whole process, and a recommendation is developed in conjunction with tax attorneys and CPAs.

Todd: Once we receive the completed analysis, we schedule a call with the client to review the tax plan and recommendations. By this time, we may have already had several calls with the client, as they like to be involved in the process of learning our structuring plans. On the second and third calls, we discuss how to drill down individually, using numbers they provided in their tax returns and questionnaire.

At this point, the client decides whether they want to engage Capital Preservation Services. If they do, we provide a basic, two-page Engagement Agreement. They pay a 20% retainer, which sets everything in motion. There is a call scheduled with one of our attorneys, usually a senior attorney such as Walt. Walt ensures we have the correct information and are ready to execute.

Walt: We then schedule the delivery of the Operational Instructions. Our concepts often start clicking on that call - our clients begin to really understand what we're attempting to accomplish. Afterward, the client pays the next 30% of the retainer.

Todd: By now, the client has received all documents and

paid 50% of the tax-deductible fee. The Implementation Phase consists of our legal team drafting documents, creating entities, and reviewing a step-by-step analysis of the strategies.

Walt: We will select the needed data to form those entities and organize the selected strategies' documentation.

This gives the client yet another overview of how the plan works and how it all fits together. Then we have a substantiation meeting. We assess the client's backup documentation, as this is a test to see how well the clients keep records and associated notes and make suggestions to assist them. There is also an introduction to the Document Assistant Program, or DAP, which provides a weekly email created by CPS. This has been a key point in positioning our clients into the habit of managing the documentation. If clients do not respond weekly, our office will contact them and ask if there is a problem that needs to be addressed or if they need additional assistance.

Todd: The client will have as many meetings with our tax attorney as necessary to engage the client in the process fully. Some clients understand the importance of substantiation right away - others are slower to come around. This depends on the client.

Walt: Once the process is complete, we move to our Offense and Defense plan. This is accomplished in a kickoff meeting, usually in the spring, where we review the previous tax year to grasp a sense of the deductions from that year. In this meeting, we roll in a plan for the *next* year, looking at what we will implement, how we will implement it, and the number of tax deductions we are looking for. We also review the client's documentation to ensure they fully understand its importance.

The year-end meeting is crucial because it will encompass many things that must be completed before the calendar year

PHASES OF THE CPS PROCESS

Gather basic client data such as age, family members, occupation and two prior tax returns.

Evaluation of client data and assessment of needs and opportunities.

Presentation of recommendations and strategy to client.

Formal engagement of Capital Preservation Services.

Presentation of **operational instructions** prepared by tax attorney.

Implementation phase, including the drafting of legal documents and formation of new corporate entities (if needed).

Substantiation meeting to review client's current documentation techniques and to explain the document assistance program.

Annual kickoff meeting to review strategy for the upcoming year.

Annual year-end meeting to ensure all strategies have been properly executed and documentation is organized and ready to file tax returns.

Audit defense plan remains in place for all CPS clients to ensure maximum preparedness in the event of an audit.

Annual customer appreciation event allows likeminded CPS clients to gather and to continue their education of opportunities as dictated by the US tax code.

ends. If we do not take those actions before the end of the year, we cannot take the deductions. We fine-tune many things for clients, such as income to flow through the qualified business income deductions. Our clients will participate in those two meetings each year under our defense plan, at a typical cost of 20% of the initial fee beginning in year two.

Todd: These two significant and powerful planning meetings tie back to the idea of playing offense vs. defense. Our clients have access to tax attorneys and CPAs throughout the year. If a client starts a new business, brings in new associates, or buys additional real estate, they can call us to advise them as to how to add those new components to their plan. There are many benefits to being with us at Capital Preservation Services, namely that our clients have high-level tax attorneys and CPAs on retainer rather than paying hourly rates to their current CPA and/or attorney.

We also provide continual updates, ideas, and articles to all our clients on a routine basis. There are 6-10 different articles released throughout the year, ranging from changes to the Tax Code to new investing ideas. The 2017 Trump Jobs and Tax Act created many changes to the Code - not only to qualified business income deductions but limits to some sole proprietor deductions. These are all planning opportunities, and as we have both said many times, if you fail to take advantage of them, you pay a lot more in taxes.

Walt: If our CPS clients are audited, we represent them through our audit defense system, including in tax court. The advantage of client representation by the tax attorneys is that they know the strategies inside and out. They can explain to the IRS representatives how the facts fit the plan, fit the Code, and why the deduction should be taken. This has been a very positive aspect of our process. If we are in front and establish that we have proper substantiation and a carefully-organized plan that adheres to the U.S. Tax Code, we can quickly knock out many issues and push the audit behind us.

Todd: That's a key advantage. Most of the time, Walt and the CPS tax attorneys know what questions the IRS will ask because they have been through the process before.

Walt: We are certainly prepared. As we move through audits, it helps us learn of items the IRS will want in advance. We can adjust our plans to accommodate. Even though the deductions fully comply with the Tax Code, we may alter a client's plan if we know we will have a particular problem with IRS auditors. We solve this problem in advance with additional paperwork, receipts, or whatever is troubling the auditor.

Lastly, we build fun into the process. We host an annual Client Appreciation Event at an attractive destination. Clients from all over the country attend, and we bring new ideas to the table. We have outside speakers, CPAs, attorneys, and other financial advisors who speak on topics like effective marketing, using social media to grow your business, developing your intellectual property, and writing books to expand your business. The biggest takeaway for many of our clients is the camaraderie of a relaxed setting, not to mention meeting new people and making connections.

Todd: Clients often ask how quickly they will see savings and tangible results. Usually, it takes 6-8 weeks compared to funding their retirement plan every month, which creates tax deductions that are not realized until a year later. At CPS, your tax savings are immediate - once the proper structures are in place, the savings begin.

To drive this point, our planning process does not work by

itself. There is no magic button - the planning requires our CPS clients *to engage* and see the savings as structural changes and mechanisms to adopt that may differ from what they have always known.

Walt: You do not have to become a CPA or tax attorney to run the process. Once your plan is in place, you will need to plan 10-20 minutes each month for additional documentation. This is documentation you should be preparing already. It can be the difference between a favorable ruling or two by the IRS and save you much money in deductions from year to year.

Todd: Between the kickoff meeting and the year-end meeting, you are looking at 2-4 hours a year with us. Our average tax savings for all CPS clients is around $60,000 a year.

CLIENT SUCCESS STORIES LEGAL REDUCTION OF MARGINAL TAX RATES

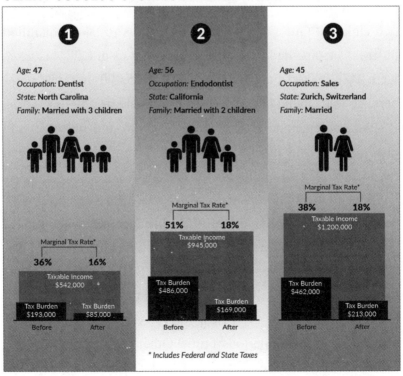

1

Age: 47
Occupation: **Dentist**
State: **North Carolina**
Family: **Married with 3 children**

Marginal Tax Rate*
36% — **16%**
Taxable Income $542,000
Tax Burden $193,000 (Before)
Tax Burden $85,000 (After)

2

Age: 56
Occupation: **Endodontist**
State: **California**
Family: **Married with 2 children**

Marginal Tax Rate*
51% — **18%**
Taxable Income $945,000
Tax Burden $486,000 (Before)
Tax Burden $169,000 (After)

3

Age: 45
Occupation: **Sales**
State: **Zurich, Switzerland**
Family: **Married**

Marginal Tax Rate*
38% — **18%**
Taxable Income $1,200,000
Tax Burden $462,000 (Before)
Tax Burden $213,000 (After)

Includes Federal and State Taxes

Clients like hearing they are saving $15,000-$30,000 per hour they spend with us.

Walt: A current client of ours is a dentist in North Carolina. He and his wife have three children. Before they joined CPS, their taxable income was $542,000, and their tax burden was $193,000. They paid 36% of his taxable income in state and federal taxes. At the time, the federal rate was 37% on a federal level, and there was an additional 5.25% from the state. The total marginal tax rate for him was 42.25%.

Once we implemented our plan, the federal and state taxes on the same amount of money fell to $85,000, or an after-tax savings of $108,000. That was in his first year of being a CPS client. Over a three-year period, it was $242,000. His average tax rate in the first year fell from 42.25% to 16%.

Another client is an endodontist in California, where they have extremely high state income taxes. He and his wife have two children. One goal we set for him was to take a qualified business income deduction. Before joining us at CPS, his taxes were $486,000 on a taxable income of $945,000. In round numbers, he was paying above 51% of his annual income in taxes.

We implemented several plans for him and indeed found qualified business income deductions for him. His tax burden fell to $169,000, dropping his tax rate to 18%.

A gentleman and his wife who have been successful with product sales from home had a taxable income of about $1.2 million and a tax burden of $462,000. They were in a 38% tax bracket when they became clients of CPS. We were able to reduce their taxes to $213,000 and reduced their rate to 18%.

With many of our strategies, you can earn a large amount of tax savings in a short period of time. Other strategies take longer to achieve the same result and realize the same deductions. We work as hard as we can to accelerate some of those deductions into your first year with us.

Todd: Finally, what is the best time of year to engage CPS? The beginning of the tax year? The middle? The end? In our opinion, the beginning of the year is best because it drives the maximum amount of tax savings. Still, those who engage us even in November or December typically see enough savings to cover our initial fee.

We hope these tips and illustrations have been helpful as you plan your own tax savings strategy. Furthermore, we hope with proper planning, thorough documentation, and sound advice from professionals, you can reduce your tax liability and create a long-term strategy to protect what you have worked so hard to earn.

12 KEY TAKEAWAYS

Your specific tax strategy takes into account all aspects of your current lifestyle, ranging from your current income level and projected time until retirement, to your number of children and whether or not they are in college or need braces. Specificity is key to a successful strategy!

Your tax strategy will involve a team of tax professionals - with a tax attorney quarterbacking the entire process.

As new opportunities and issues reveal themselves throughout the year, you can review them against your current tax plan with the help of your team of professionals so that the best possible decisions are made.

Your time investment in executing your tax strategy should be approximately 10-20 minutes per month, and 2-4 hours per year. When weighed against your tax savings, this will likely prove to be the most profitable investment of your time each year!

Your can begin experiencing tax savings within weeks of implementing your plan, and in most instances, your fees are more than covered by your savings.

▶ VIDEO RESOURCES

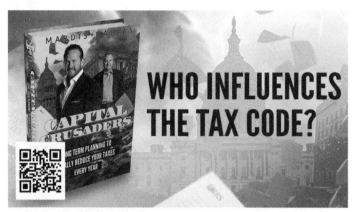

LINK: bit.ly/Crusaders14

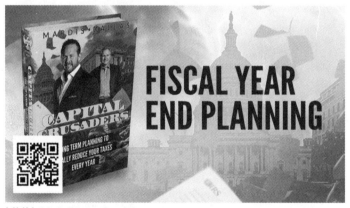

LINK: bit.ly/Crusaders33

For more information on long-term planning to legally reduce your taxes every year, please visit Capital Preservation Services online at:

CPSLLCMS.COM